The
CLOCK WATCHER'S
COOKBOOK

The
CLOCK WATCHER'S
COOKBOOK

by
Judy Duncan
&
Allison McCance

YANKEE BOOKS

A division of Yankee Publishing Incorporated, Dublin, New Hampshire

Design by John White
Illustrations by Erick Ingraham

Yankee Publishing Incorporated
Dublin, New Hampshire
First Edition
Copyright 1983, by Yankee Publishing Incorporated

Library of Congress Catalogue Card No. 82-63133
ISBN: 0-89909-013-3

We'd like to thank our friend Claudie Malone for her insights and encouragement with this book.

Table of Contents

Introduction

TAKE the best recipes of two lifelong friends who love to cook and entertain, combine with clear, specific directions, season with time-saving shortcuts, add thorough kitchen testing, and the result is this book.

While we enjoy creating a wide variety of foods, we are also busy with families, careers, carpools, and sports. Consequently, we don't have the time or the desire to live in the kitchen. Speed and convenience are important. Many of our recipes can be made in twenty minutes or less; over seventy dishes can be readied in ten minutes. All of the recipes are aimed at reducing kitchen time to sixty minutes or less.

We have given realistic, not idealis-tic, preparation and cooking times for all recipes. We have written clear directions to encourage the inexperienced cook, have included a Recipe Timetable, and have cross-referenced our recipes into six helpful categories: last-minute dishes (from cupboard to table in under 30 minutes), recipes that are quick to prepare (5, 10, 15 minutes), those that adapt to microwave cooking, those that can be made ahead and frozen, as well as recipes that are suited for the calorie conscious and those that are temptations for any chocolate lover. Most items are made from scratch. Many are quick, easy, and elegant; others require more effort. To help you fit them into a busy schedule, we have given timesaving tips on their preparation. We have also included a checklist for planning a large dinner party and sample menus for various special occasions.

To reduce kitchen time and effort, we often turn to those great labor-saving appliances — microwave oven, electric frying pan, food processor, blender. Although use of these appliances for our recipes is optional, we offer you the benefits of our experience with them to help you decide if and when you might want to acquire them.

The Microwave Oven

Although designed for a regular oven, some of our recipes are equally successful, and much quicker, when cooked in the microwave oven. For example, the cooking time for Easy Pork in Wine or for Lemon Meringue Squares can be halved when using a microwave. These recipes are starred in the Recipe Timetable, and directions for both methods of cooking are included.

Microwaving is a quick way to heat, reheat, or cook food. The frantic chef will find some aspects of microwave cooking invaluable. The microwave is useful for quickly defrosting foods and good for heating staggered meals when diners eat at different times. Leftover casseroles can be divided into convenient serving sizes, labeled and dated, frozen in heavy-duty plastic storage bags (never use aluminum foil), and reheated quickly (be sure to poke a few holes in the bag

so steam can escape). Moist foods such as fish, chicken, and vegetables can be cooked in a microwave oven more successfully than dry foods. Moist cakes bake well. Melting squares of baking chocolate in their paper is handy. Frozen vegetables need no extra water, which enhances flavor and nutrition. The microwave is also good for blanching fresh vegetables before freezing and for crisping soggy crackers and chips.

However, microwaving does not do well with all foods. Meat comes out gray unless specially treated either by browning it first or by coating it with glaze, crumbs, or paprika. Reheating muffins can dry them out. Many dishes require more attention with a microwave than with conventional cooking. A mere thirty seconds of overcooking can ruin a meal. Sometimes it's easier to let a pot simmer in a conventional oven unattended for a longer period of time. Cooking large amounts of food in a microwave is inconvenient because the amount of food being cooked directly affects the cooking time. One baked potato takes six minutes; four take twenty minutes (and several rotations, unless your microwave is a newer model that doesn't require rotating). Our recipes calling for six pork chops would be a nuisance to microwave, whereas our two-chop recipe works fine.

The shape of food and its placement in the oven will affect speed and evenness of cooking. Geometric objects like bar cookies and brownies cook well. Circular placement of foods in the oven also helps. Therefore, freeze leftovers in even, thin, preferably circular shapes.

One more caution: never use metal of any sort, including a plate with decorative gold or silver trim, in a microwave oven. Metal causes arcing and can ruin the oven. China, ceramic, glass, plastic, or paper containers are fine. Many containers and packaging products are so labeled if they are microwave safe. Plastic wrap or wax paper covers prevent splattering.

We have added directions for microwave cooking, including timing, arrangement, and rotation, where we feel they will facilitate preparation without sacrificing flavor. For example, Quick Picnic Chicken could be done in a microwave, but the flavor is markedly inferior to that produced by conventional oven cooking.

Our oven is 650 watts, which is the most common kind. If your model is less than 600 watts, cooking times should be increased; if it is over 700 watts, times should be decreased. Microwaving can be a great convenience and timesaver, but we have found it to be a good supplement to, rather than a substitute for, cooking with a conventional range and oven.

The Electric Frying Pan

An electric frying pan is especially useful when range space is limited. Many pans are large and offer a wide, even cooking area designed for efficient volume cooking. Some are attractive and designed for cooking or warming food at a buffet table. Pans come with dome covers and are good for long-term simmering since the thermostat works with fine gradations of heat, like the "sensi-temp" feature found on some stoves. Many pans are deep and can be used for semi-deep-fat frying.

In addition to being convenient, the frying pan can be a low-cost alternative to oven cooking.

Many electric pans warm up higher than the designated temperature and then cut back to the desired thermostat setting. Therefore, preheat the pan 100° lower than wanted, and after eight minutes turn up the temperature. Some pans, like some ovens, are inaccurate in their settings — usually erring on the warm side. Experiment with your pan, learn its temperature quirks, and adjust accordingly. Also, be careful to keep the pan handle and cord away from the counter's edge and out of reach of small children and pets.

We find an electric frying pan to be especially useful for pancakes, French Toast, Buttermilk Puffs, stews, soups, Coq au Vin, Better Baked Beans, Shrimp Tempura, and Cheese Velvet.

The Food Processor

The food processor is a timesaving, efficient, and versatile kitchen aid. It speeds up slicing, dicing, chopping, kneading, and blending of many foods, especially when large amounts are needed. Many of its tasks can be done by a blender, grater, or a set of good knives, but the food processor is faster and it produces uniformly good results.

As with any appliance, study your instruction book carefully. Learn its important safety precautions and how to use your machine's individual accessories. Note that the machine will not whip egg whites or cream.

Processors have a variety of blades and disks. Some come with the machine, and others are sold separately. Here is a sampling:

• The standard *metal blade*, also known as a steel knife, is essential for chopping, mincing, puréeing, and grating hard substances such as meat, cheese, ice (very noisy), and nuts. However, grinding coffee beans will permanently scratch the bowl.

> *For a coarse chop*: turn machine on and off quickly. Onions cut in quarters chop well by this method, but they don't brown as well when sautéed as do hand-cut onions.
> *For fine blending*: keep the motor running continuously. To mince garlic, drop the clove(s) through the funnel opening with the blade already running.
> *As a dough hook*: it kneads dough in seconds and cuts a delicious pie crust in less than a minute.

• The *plastic blade* is used for mixing softer substances such as tuna salad and for blending liquids. When you are making soups or a liquid batter, as in Blender Maple Pancakes, hold the blade down on the bottom shaft with your index finger to avoid spills when you are removing the bowl from the motor and pouring the batter out of the bowl. Usually two cups is the bowl's optimal liquid capacity.

• Disks can include slicers, shredders, julienne disks, and a cutter for French fried potatoes. We have found the medium slicer and medium shredder to be the most useful optional accessories. Don't try to shred hard or medium-hard cheese; it can crack the plastic shaft. After Swiss cheese damaged one disk's shaft, we learned to cut the cheese in chunks first and grate them with the steel blade.

The following tips can be handy when using your accessories:
> Make sure carrots are at room temperature before slicing.

> To julienne zucchini and carrots with a medium slicer disk, cut to funnel width, lay the vegetables horizontally in the funnel opening, and slice, then reslice the resulting long slices sideways.

> To dice celery, cut stalks to plunger length and stack them lengthwise in the funnel opening so that the blade cuts across the grain.

> To cut apples for pies or tarts, use the medium slicer. To slice mushrooms, stack them sideways in the funnel opening.

To eliminate extra cleanup when using the food processor for several steps, start with dry ingredients and work through to moister ones, rather than following the order listed in a recipe. For example, ingredients in Fancy Herb Chicken Casserole include sliced mushrooms, chopped onions, and shredded cheese. Shred the cheese first, slice the mushrooms, and then chop the onions.

The Blender

The electric blender can do many of the jobs of a food processor's steel knife and some the processor cannot do. The blender works very well in mixing liquids, puréeing solids and liquids, mixing semi-soft ingredients, grating bread and hard cheese, chopping nuts, and grinding coffee beans. Because the blender can work at low speeds, it can whip cream quickly and blend a light, delicious hollandaise sauce.

Like the food processor, the blender rapidly purées solids mixed with liquids for soups. After careful and thorough mixing on high, pour the purée through a sieve. This is a lot easier than using a hand food mill or mashing food through a sieve by hand. Do small batches at a time. Fill the container only halfway and keep it covered. If it is necessary to push down ingredients with the motor running, do not use a metal tool and never push down too close to the blades, or you too might end up with Béarnaise sauce on the kitchen ceiling.

The blender can fine-grind nuts in smaller amounts than a processor can. A hand grinder would also work well. Coarse chopping is better left to a processor or chopping knife.

The blender grates small amounts of fresh bread crumbs well. Do one slice at a time, breaking bread into fourths. Turn blender on high. Of course, fresh bread crumbs can still be made by placing a slice flat on a board and lightly pulling it into crumbs with a fork.

In addition to the fresh bread and cracker crumbs used in several recipes, the blender expedites making Cashew Cookies, Minted Pea and Fresh Tomato Soups, and Eggnog Trifle. Blender Maple Pancakes, Hollandaise and Béarnaise sauces, Quick Chocolate Pots de Crème, and Kahlua Cheesecake can be made completely in the blender.

Giving a Large Party

The large cocktail party is a time-honored way of paying back a lot of people in one fell swoop and safely mixing several different groups together. It can be a lot of work, but experience, planning, and preparing food ahead can keep you relaxed enough to enjoy your guests. Here are some tips that will help you entertain with elegance as well as ease.

Set up the bar away from the food to avoid overcrowding an area. Fill large platters with hors d'oeuvres and double recipes for molds and dips to avoid frequent refills. Plan to serve hot hors d'oeuvres that can be cooked early and kept on a hot tray to keep kitchen time and concern over food to a minimum.

As a general rule of thumb, we recommend seven hors d'oeuvres per person, 1½ ounces of rich cheese, like Brie, per person, or if serving sliced cold cuts, ¼ pound per person. If you aren't sure about how many people are coming, have extra supplies of cheese and crackers or nuts as a backup.

Planning ahead is important for just about any kind or size of gathering. For a large, formal dinner party, start your planning well in advance so that last-minute preparations are kept to a minimum. The following checklist provides step-by-step suggestions, beginning a full month ahead of time.

Party Planning Checklist

1 MONTH AHEAD:
Choose type and size of party.
Order extra chairs, tables, linen, etc.
Plan parking.
Mail or phone invitations.

3 WEEKS AHEAD:
List names of guests to record RSVPs.
Plan menu.
a) Check for contrasts in taste, color, and texture. (A terrible menu would be Swiss Scallops, Creamy Potatoes, Hasty Corn Pudding, and Banana Cream Pie. See p. 15 for some good suggestions.)
b) Include as many items as possible that can be made ahead.
c) Plan cooking times — do not try to bake two things at different temperatures in one oven at the same time.
d) Consider food allergies or strong dislikes your guests may have.
Coordinate decorations with color scheme — linen, candles, centerpieces, napkins, etc.
Buy beverages — liquor, mixers, soft drinks.

2 WEEKS AHEAD:
Make grocery lists.
Purchase supplies for make-ahead dishes.
Begin preparing foods to be frozen.
Label completed dishes and check off on menu.

1 WEEK AHEAD:
Plan seating arrangements.
Choose your wardrobe — clean and press if necessary.
Clean your house — don't leave any area messy.
Finish preparing frozen foods.

4-5 DAYS AHEAD:
Put extra hangers in coat closet and/or freshen guest room.
Write place cards.

2-3 DAYS AHEAD:
Buy fresh fruits, vegetables, meats, and perishable bar condiments.
Make dishes that can be prepared ahead.
Write out detailed timetable — when to preheat oven, cook various foods, chill wine, warm dessert, etc.

1 DAY AHEAD:
Set table — do any necessary polishing and ironing.
Put out serving dishes, platters, hot plates.

DAY OF PARTY:
Get flowers and extra ice.
Prepare last-minute food; defrost, warm, unmold, or decorate remaining dishes.
Go over bathrooms, guest room, and coat closet again.
Feed and wash young children.

Allow half an hour before party to give directions to any helping hands you may have.

This book has recipes covering many ways of feeding a family and entertaining guests. Since preparation and cooking times are given in the Recipe Timetable, and we have cross-referenced lists as well (see pp. 26-30), planning menus primarily by the clock is easy. Keeping in mind the importance of contrasts in taste, color, and texture, we have included some quick, delicious menus (for a variety of occasions), which can be prepared and cooked in less than an hour.

Menu
Suggestions

Brunch

I	II
Grapes & Kirsch	Orange Juice
Poached Omelet	Delicate Corn
Light Lemon	Cakes
Coffee Cake	Apple Walnut
Tea and Coffee	Streusel
	Bacon and
	Sausage
	Tea and Coffee

Lunch

I	II
Delicious Vegetable	Single Seafood
Soup	Salad
Baked Alaska	Blueberry Muffins
Crab Sandwich	Gogol Mogul
Pineapple Garni	

Tea

I	II
Lemon Nut Muffins	Broccoli Canapés
Spicy Chip Cookies	Cheese with
Frosted Oatmeal	Fines Herbes
Cookies	Mushroom
	Rounds

Cocktails

I	II
Artichoke Balls	Betsy's Shrimp
Guacamole	Cocktail
Cheese Fingers	Crab Dip
	Crisp Cheese
	Crackers

Dinner

I	II
Elegant Mushroom	Zucchini Soup
Consommé	Sherried Shad Roe
Filet of Beef	Crunchy Green
en Papillote	Beans
Citrus Carrots	Zabaglione
Green Salad	
Quick Chocolate	
Pots de Crème	

Recipe Timetable

Breakfast or Brunch

Muffins	Cook Time	Prep. Time
32 — Look n' Cook Maple Bran Muffins	10 min.	15 min.*
33 — Everyday Apple Oatmeal Muffins	10 min.	15 min.*
33 — Orange Pecan Muffins	10 min.	20 min.
34 — Banana Bran Muffins	15 min.	20 min.
34 — Blueberry Muffins	10 min.	25 min.

Coffee Cakes		
34 — Sweet Blueberry Coffee Cake	10 min.	55 min.
35 — Light Lemon Coffee Cake	10 min.	45 min.
35 — Full-Meal Coffee Cake	30 min.	1 hr. & 15 min.
36 — Almond Coffee Cake	25 min.	40 min.
36 — Apple Walnut Streusel	20 min.	30 min.

Pancakes, Eggs, and Toast		
37 — Blender Maple Pancakes	5 min.	6 min.*
38 — Fruit Yogurt Pancakes	10 min.	6 min.*
38 — Swedish Pancakes	5 min.	6 min.*
39 — Banana Pancakes	5 min.	6 min.*
39 — Delicate Corn Cakes	5 min.	10 min.*
40 — Buttermilk Puffs	15 min.	15 min.
40 — Shirred Eggs	5 min.	10 min.
40 — Poached Omelet	10 min.	15 min.
41 — French Toast	5 min.	10 min.
41 — Jam Toast	5 min.	10 min.

* Cooking time will be greatly reduced with a microwave oven. Special instructions for using a microwave are given in these recipes.
+ Additional time required for marinating, simmering, chilling, etc.

Luncheon or Supper

Soups and Sandwiches	Cook Time	Prep. Time
42 — Light Moussaka Soup	20 min.	30 min.
43 — Vermont Butternut Soup	20 min.	45 min.
43 — Easy Carrot Soup	35 min.	1 hr.
43 — Delicious Vegetable Soup	20 min.	30 min.
44 — Sonny's Onion Soup	45 min.	30 min.
44 — Potato Potage	30 min.	10 min.
45 — Jack's Reuben Sandwich	10 min.	6 min.
45 — Baked Alaska Crab Sandwich	15 min.	20 min.*

Cheeses and Quiches		
46 — Basic Food Processor Pie Crust Dough	5 min.	—
46 — Butter Pie Crust Dough	10 min.	—
46 — Cheese Velvet	10 min.	30 min.*
47 — Alpine Cheese Fondue	5 min.	10 min.
47 — Special Quiche Lorraine	15 min.	40 min.
47 — Crustless Quiche	10 min.	30 min.*
48 — Sherried Turkey Quiche	15 min.	40 min.
48 — Mushroom or Artichoke Tart	30 min.	35 min.

Salads and Molds		
49 — Chicken Salad with Cashews	15 min.	—
49 — Single Seafood Salad	10 min.	—
49 — Simple Salmon Mousse	5 min.	chill 2 hr.
50 — Slimming Strawberry Mousse	10 min.	chill 4 hr.
51 — Avocado Chutney Ring	10 min.	chill 4 hr.
51 — Diet Asparagus Mold	10 min.	chill 4 hr.
51 — Foolproof Tomato Aspic	15 min.	chill 3 hr.
52 — Minted Fruit Mold	20 min.	chill 3 hr.

* Cooking time will be greatly reduced with a microwave oven. Special instructions for using a microwave are given in these recipes.
+ Additional time required for marinating, simmering, chilling, etc.

Meats and Casseroles

	Cook Time	Prep. Time
52 — Modern Turkey Divan	20 min.	15 min.
53 — Better Baked Beans	30 min.	45 min.
53 — Dashing Hamburger Casserole	20 min.	30 min.
53 — Apple Meat Loaf	10 min.	1 hr.
54 — Meatball Stroganoff	30 min.	15 min.
54 — Precooked Sausage Shish Kebab	30 min.	10 min.

Breads

55 — Apple Tea Bread	25 min.	50 min.
55 — Zucchini Bread	20 min.	1 hr.
56 — Southern Corn Bread	15 min.	45 min.*
56 — Cranberry Orange Bread	30 min.	50 min.
57 — Herbed Popovers	10 min.	20 min.
57 — Banana Bread	20 min.	55 min.
57 — Lemon Nut Muffins	20 min.	20 min.

Snacks

Cookies and Brownies

60 — Spicy Chip Cookies	10 min.	6 min.
60 — Peanut Butterscotch Cookies	15 min.	8 min.
61 — Cashew Cookies	15 min.	20 min.
61 — Rum Pecan Puffs	15 min.	18 min.
61 — Lemon Meringue Squares	20 min.	30 min.*
62 — Brandied Pecan Mini-Tarts	40 min.	23 min.
62 — Frosted Oatmeal Cookies	30 min.+	10 min.
63 — Chocolate Hip Huggers	20 min.	12 min.
64 — Sociable Hermits	10 min.+	8 min.
64 — Creamy Orange Cookies	15 min.	8 min.
65 — Blueberry Bars	20 min.	40 min.
65 — Helen's Heavenly Nutmeats	10 min.	30 min.

* Cooking time will be greatly reduced with a microwave oven. Special instructions for using a microwave are given in these recipes.
+ Additional time required for marinating, simmering, chilling, etc.

	Cook Time	Prep. Time
65 — Blond Brownies	15 min.	35 min.*
66 — Fudge Brownies	20 min.	25 min.*
66 — Chocolate Mint Meringues	10 min.	20 min.
67 — Mocha Meringues	10 min.	20 min.

Cocktails

Hot Appetizers

68 — Jamaican Bacon	15 min.	15 min.*
69 — Clams Casino	15 min.	5 min.
69 — Gruyère Cubes	30 min.	8 min.
70 — Zucchini Figures	15 min.	25 min.
70 — Crab Puffs	25 min.	12 min.*
71 — Bacon Crisps	10 min.	30 min.
71 — Chutney Cheese Canapés	10 min.	5 min.
71 — Crab Dip	10 min.	20 min.*
72 — Clam Dip	10 min.	30 min.
72 — Miniature Quiches	30 min.	15 min.
72 — Potato Crisps	5 min.	8 min.
73 — Impulse Cheese Dip	5 min.	15 min.*
73 — Cheese Fingers	10 min.	10 min.
73 — Mushroom Rounds	20 min.	10 min.

Cold Appetizers

74 — Shrimp Cocktail Mousse	25 min.	chill 4 hr.
74 — Caviar Mold	15 min.	chill 4 hr.
75 — Party Artichokes and Shrimp ...	40 min.	—
75 — Broccoli Canapés	15 min.	—
75 — Cherry Tomato Canapés	30 min.	chill 2 hr.
75 — Guacamole	10 min.	—
76 — Pâté with Currants and Cognac .	20 min.	chill 2 hr.

* Cooking time will be greatly reduced with a microwave oven. Special instructions
for using a microwave are given in these recipes.
+ Additional time required for marinating, simmering, chilling, etc.

* Cooking time will be greatly reduced with a microwave oven. Special instructions for using a microwave are given in these recipes.
+ Additional time required for marinating, simmering, chilling, etc.

	Cook Time	Prep. Time
87 — Complete Chicken Casserole	30 min.	45 min.
87 — Chicken with Avocado and Almonds	20 min.	45 min.
88 — Coq au Vin	20 min.	35 min.
89 — Family Favorite Fowl	10 min.	35 min.
89 — Chicken Cordon Rouge	30 min.	35 min.*
90 — Quick Picnic Chicken	10 min.	1 hr.
90 — Chicken with Wine and Tomatoes	25 min.	45 min.
91 — Easy Pork in Wine	10 min.	45 min.
91 — Barbecued Pork Ribs	20 min.+	8 min.
91 — Pork and Peaches	15 min.	50 min.
92 — Pork Tenderloin with Cointreau	15 min.	45 min.
92 — Sherried Pork Chops	5 min.	1 hr.
92 — Baked Ham with Maple and Port	10 min.	1 hr.
93 — Ham and Green Bean Casserole	15 min.+	50 min.

Fish and Seafood

	Cook Time	Prep. Time
93 — Sherried Shad Roe	5 min.	20 min.
93 — Shrimp Tempura	20 min.	10 min.
94 — Sensational Swordfish or Scrod	5 min.	10 min.*
94 — Georgian Shrimp Casserole	20 min.	55 min.
94 — Saffron Shrimp	15 min.	1 hr.
95 — Louisiana Shrimp	20 min.	30 min.
95 — Crab Casserole	30 min.	40 min.
96 — Swiss Scallops	10 min.	5 min.

Vegetables

	Cook Time	Prep. Time
96 — Hasty Corn Pudding	5 min.	45 min.*
96 — Crunchy Green Beans	15 min.	30 min.
97 — Peas Alaska	15 min.	5 min.

* Cooking time will be greatly reduced with a microwave oven. Special instructions for using a microwave are given in these recipes.
+ Additional time required for marinating, simmering, chilling, etc.

Desserts

Fruit, Mousse, Soufflés, Etc.

* Cooking time will be greatly reduced with a microwave oven. Special instructions for using a microwave are given in these recipes.
+ Additional time required for marinating, simmering, chilling, etc.

	Cook Time	Prep. Time
109 — Double Orange Soufflé	15 min.	1 hr.
109 — Chocolate Bombe	20 min.	chill 1 hr.
109 — Hot Fudge Sauce	5 min.	5 min.
110 — Butter Almond Bombe	20 min.	chill 1 hr.
110 — Butterscotch Sauce	5 min.	6 min.
110 — Pineapple Rum Ice Cream	15 min.	chill 1 hr.
111 — Coffee Ice Cream Mold	10 min.	chill 1 hr.
111 — Zabaglione	10 min.	10 min.
111 — Gogol Mogul	10 min.	—

Cakes

	Cook Time	Prep. Time
111 — Mrs. Erickson's Red Velvet Cake	40 min.	30 min.
112 — White Velvet Frosting	20 min.	—
112 — Self-Frosted Chocolate Almond Cake	10 min.	30 min.
112 — Kahlua Cheesecake	50 min.	chill 4 hr.
113 — Hawaiian Carrot Cake	30 min.	1 hr. & 15 min.
113 — Coconut Icing	10 min.	—
114 — Marble Cake	20 min.	30 min.
114 — 5-Minute Chocolate Icing	5 min.	—
114 — Applesauce Cake	15 min.	30 min.
115 — Rich Chocolate Cake	15 min.	30 min.
115 — Fudge Mint Frosting	10 min.	—

Pies

	Cook Time	Prep. Time
115 — French Apple Tarts	20 min.	1 hr.
116 — Strawberry Cheese Pie	30 min.+	chill 1 hr.
116 — Midnight Mousse Pie	25 min.	chill 2 hr.
116 — Coconut Cream Pie	30 min.+	15 min.*

* Cooking time will be greatly reduced with a microwave oven. Special instructions for using a microwave are given in these recipes.

+ Additional time required for marinating, simmering, chilling, etc.

* Cooking time will be greatly reduced with a microwave oven. Special instructions for using a microwave are given in these recipes.
+ Additional time required for marinating, simmering, chilling, etc.

Special Recipes

Quick Preparation — 15 Minutes

Last-Minute Dishes

From Cupboard to Table in Under 30 Minutes

Microwave Meals

Make-Ahead Favorites

For the Calorie Conscious

For Chocolate Lovers

Breakfast or Brunch

Muffins

Look n' Cook Maple Bran Muffins

Prep. 10 min. Cook 15 min. Makes 2½ dozen.

An easy way to have fresh breakfast muffins any day for up to a month.

1 cup 100% bran cereal

1 cup boiling water

⅔ cup margarine

1½ cups brown sugar (light, dark, or brownulated)

2 eggs, well beaten

2 cups fresh buttermilk

¼ cup maple syrup

2 cups flour

1 tablespoon baking soda

½ cup wheat germ

2¼ cups bran buds

Preheat oven to 400°. Soak 100% bran cereal in boiling water and set aside. Cream margarine and sugar in a large bowl. Blend in beaten eggs, buttermilk, softened cereal, and maple syrup. Sift flour and soda together and mix gently into batter. Stir in wheat germ and bran buds.

Spoon batter into well-greased muffin pans, filling each cup two-thirds full. Bake for 15 minutes or until a toothpick inserted in the center comes out clean.

Make Ahead: To enjoy fresh muffins each morning, put batter in an airtight container and refrigerate for as long as a month. Bake muffins as desired. Cooked muffins freeze well in airtight wrap.

Microwave: Lightly grease 3 custard cups and put paper liners inside cups. Fill each half full with batter. Arrange in a circle. Cook on high for 2 minutes 45 seconds. For one muffin, cook on high for 1 minute 45 seconds.

Everyday Apple Oatmeal Muffins

Prep. 10 min. Cook 15 min. Makes 2½ dozen.

A fine flavor combination that's ready in minutes.

½ cup plus 2 tablespoons margarine
1½ cups sugar
2 eggs, well beaten
1 cup unsweetened applesauce
2 cups fresh buttermilk
2½ cups flour
2 teaspoons cinnamon
1 tablespoon baking soda
½ teaspoon salt
2 cups quick-cooking oats
1 cup raisins (optional)

Preheat oven to 400°. Cream margarine and sugar thoroughly in a large bowl. Blend in well-beaten eggs, add applesauce, and beat in buttermilk. Sift flour, cinnamon, soda, and salt together. Mix into batter. Add oats and mix thoroughly. Stir in raisins if desired.

Spoon batter into well-greased muffin pans, filling each cup two-thirds full. Bake for 15-18 minutes or until toothpick inserted in center comes out clean.

Make Ahead: Batter can be stored for up to a month in an airtight container in the refrigerator; fresh muffins can be baked when desired. Cooked muffins freeze well in airtight wrap.

Microwave: Lightly grease 3 custard cups and put paper liners inside cups. Fill each half full with batter. Arrange in circle. Cook on high for 2 minutes 45 seconds. For one muffin, cook on high for 1 minute 45 seconds.

Orange Pecan Muffins

Prep. 10 min. Cook 20 min. Makes 16.

Guests always ask for this recipe.

2 cups less 2 tablespoons flour
5 tablespoons sugar
1 tablespoon baking powder
½ teaspoon salt
½ teaspoon cinnamon
½ cup coarsely chopped pecans
1 egg
¼ cup vegetable oil
½ cup orange juice
1 teaspoon vanilla
½ cup milk

Preheat oven to 375°. Sift together dry ingredients into a large bowl. Add chopped pecans. In a separate bowl beat egg and oil until light and foamy. Add juice, vanilla, and milk to egg mixture. Pour liquids into dry ingredients. Stir with a spoon only enough to blend ingredients. Batter will still be slightly lumpy. Spoon batter into greased muffin pan, filling each cup two-thirds full. Bake for 20-25 minutes or until a toothpick inserted in the center comes out clean.

Make Ahead: Muffins keep fresh

for a day. They also freeze well. Warm frozen muffins at 350° for 20 minutes.

Banana Bran Muffins

Prep. 15 min. Cook 20 min. Makes 1 dozen.

A tasty fruit-and-cereal mixture. The banana flavor hides the fact that bran is good for you.

¼ cup butter or margarine
½ cup light brown sugar
1 egg
2 cups mashed bananas (4 medium)
1½ cups raisin bran cereal
2 teaspoons vanilla
2 tablespoons honey (optional)
1½ cups flour
2 teaspoons baking powder
½ teaspoon salt
1 teaspoon baking soda

Preheat oven to 350°. In a large bowl cream butter and sugar together until fluffy. Beat in egg. Blend in bananas, cereal, vanilla, and honey if desired. Sift dry ingredients together and stir them gently into batter. Do not overmix. Batter should still be slightly lumpy. Spoon mixture into greased muffin pan, filling each cup two-thirds full.

Bake for 20-25 minutes. Muffins are cooked when a toothpick inserted in the center comes out clean.

Make Ahead: Muffins freeze well. Thaw and warm when ready to serve.

Blueberry Muffins

Prep. 10 min. Cook 25 min. Makes 1 dozen.

A quick, zesty version of an all-time favorite.

1 cup blueberries
1½ tablespoons sugar
⅓ cup butter or margarine
⅓ cup sugar
1 egg
1 teaspoon vanilla
1½ cups sifted flour
1 tablespoon baking powder
½ teaspoon cinnamon
⅔ cup milk

Preheat oven to 400°. Toss blueberries in 1½ tablespoons sugar and set aside. Beat butter, ⅓ cup sugar, egg, and vanilla together until light and fluffy. Sift dry ingredients together and add in thirds to batter alternately with milk. Beat well after each addition. Stir in blueberries.

Grease 12 muffin cups and fill two-thirds full with batter. Bake for 25 minutes or until lightly browned and firm to the touch. Loosen edges with a knife and carefully remove from pan.

Make Ahead: Muffins freeze well if cooled and wrapped in foil or stored in airtight container. Warm at 350° for 15 minutes before serving. Refrigerated muffins remain fresh for a day.

Coffee Cakes

Sweet Blueberry Coffee Cake

Prep. 10 min. Cook 55 min. Serves 12.

Blueberry yogurt is the mystery ingredient in this very moist and easy-to-prepare cake.

2 tablespoons sugar
1 package (18½ ounces) yellow or
  white cake mix
2 tablespoons flour
¾ cup vegetable oil
4 eggs
1 cup blueberry yogurt

Do not preheat oven. In a large bowl combine sugar, cake mix, flour, and oil. Add eggs and beat batter for 4 minutes. Mix in yogurt. Pour batter into a large, well-greased bundt pan, allowing space for batter to rise. Place cake in a *cold* oven and bake at 325° for 55 minutes. Cake is done when an ice pick inserted in the center comes out clean. After cake has cooled for about 10 minutes, loosen sides with a knife and invert carefully onto a plate.

Make Ahead: Cake freezes well if wrapped in foil or plastic wrap. Thaw and serve. Good either warm or cool.

Light Lemon Coffee Cake

Prep. 10 min. Cook 45 min. Serves 12.

The sweet, tangy flavor is so appealing that this can also be a dessert cake.

1 package (18½ ounces) white cake
  mix
1 package (3¾ ounces) instant lemon
  pudding
4 eggs
¾ cup water
⅔ cup vegetable oil
1 tablespoon lemon juice

¼ teaspoon grated lemon rind
Topping (see below)

Preheat oven to 350°. Place cake mix, pudding, eggs, water, oil, lemon juice, and rind in a large bowl. Beat together at medium-high speed for 4 minutes, until well mixed. Pour batter into greased bundt pan. Bake for 45-50 minutes or until an ice pick inserted in the center comes out clean. Cool for 10 minutes, loosen edges with a knife, and invert carefully onto a plate. Drizzle with topping.

Topping
¼ cup confectioners sugar
1 tablespoon milk
½ teaspoon lemon juice
¼ teaspoon grated lemon rind

Mix all ingredients together, blending thoroughly.

Make Ahead: Cake still tastes fresh after 4 days of refrigeration. Heat at 350° for 5-10 minutes until warm. Freezes well: place on a plate in the freezer for 30 minutes, then wrap tightly in foil. Serve at room temperature.

Full-Meal Coffee Cake

Prep. 30 min. Cook 1 hr. 15 min. Serves 16.

All the ingredients for a complete breakfast in every slice.

1 pound bulk sausage
1 cup light brown sugar
1 cup white sugar
4 eggs
3¼ cups flour
½ teaspoon ginger
1 tablespoon cinnamon
¼ teaspoon nutmeg

⅛ teaspoon ground cloves
1 teaspoon instant coffee granules
1 teaspoon baking powder
1 teaspoon baking soda
1 cup orange juice
1 cup crispy rice cereal
1 cup raisins (optional)
1 tablespoon confectioners sugar

Preheat oven to 350°. In a large bowl mix sausage and brown and white sugars. Beat in eggs and blend until mixture is light. Sift flour, spices, coffee, baking powder, and soda together. Alternate adding flour mixture and orange juice to sausage batter, blending well after each addition. Fold in cereal and raisins, if desired.

Pour batter into a 9-cup bundt pan that has been greased and dusted with 1 tablespoon confectioners sugar. Bake for 1 hour 15 minutes. Cake is done when cake tester inserted in the center comes out clean. Cool in pan for 10 minutes, loosen sides, and invert carefully onto a plate.

Make Ahead: Cake freezes well if cooled and wrapped tightly in foil. Cake can be stored in the refrigerator for a week.

Almond Coffee Cake

Prep. 25 min. Cook 40 min. Serves 8-10.

A good buttery nut flavor to complement your breakfast.

½ cup butter or margarine
1 cup white sugar
2 eggs
½ teaspoon almond extract
½ teaspoon vanilla extract
2 cups flour

1 teaspoon baking soda
1 teaspoon baking powder
½ teaspoon salt
1 cup unflavored yogurt

Topping
2 tablespoons butter or margarine
¼ cup light brown sugar
½ cup sliced almonds

Preheat oven to 350°. Cream ½ cup butter and white sugar until light and fluffy. Add eggs one at a time, beating for a minute after each addition. Add extracts. Sift dry ingredients and add alternately to the batter with the yogurt. Grease and dust with flour a 9″ pie pan or a small bundt pan.

In a separate bowl make topping: mix butter, brown sugar, and almonds together. Layer one-third of the batter in the baking pan. Cover with one-third of the topping. Repeat layers of batter and topping twice more.

Bake for 40 minutes or until a toothpick inserted in the center comes out clean.

Make Ahead: Cake remains fresh in the refrigerator for two days; it also freezes well if tightly wrapped in foil after cooling.

Apple Walnut Streusel

Prep. 20 min. Cook 30 min. Serves 8-10.

A pretty cake that is both moist and crunchy.

¼ cup butter or margarine
½ cup sugar
1 egg
1 teaspoon vanilla
2 teaspoons baking powder

2 cups flour

¾ cup milk

Topping

2 tablespoons light brown sugar

2 tablespoons melted butter or margarine

4 tablespoons flour

2 teaspoons cinnamon

1 cup chopped walnuts

1 medium McIntosh apple, peeled, cored, and thinly sliced

Preheat oven to 350°. Cream butter and sugar until light and fluffy. Beat in egg and vanilla. Sift baking powder with flour, then sift by thirds into batter alternately with the milk, blending well after each addition.

In a separate bowl make the topping: stir together the brown sugar, melted butter, flour, cinnamon, and nuts. Pour half of the coffee cake batter into a greased 9"-10" pie pan. Spread half of the streusel topping evenly over cake. Arrange apple slices in concentric circles on top. Pour the remaining batter over the apples and cover with remaining topping. Bake for 30-40 minutes until lightly browned.

Make Ahead: Cake stays fresh for 2 days in the refrigerator. Cake also freezes well if covered tightly with foil.

Pancakes, Eggs, and Toast

Blender Maple Pancakes

Prep. 5 min. Cook 6 min. Serves 4.

Quick as a mix and twice as good.

1½ teaspoons vegetable oil or butter

2 eggs

1½ cups flour, pre-sifted or "instantized" (like Wondra)

½ teaspoon salt

1 tablespoon baking powder

1 cup milk

¼ cup maple syrup

Spread oil over bottom of a large frying pan and warm over medium-high heat (about 375°). Blend all other ingredients at high speed in a blender for 1 minute. Turn off motor, remove cover, and stir batter. Blend for another minute until batter is smooth. Pour ¼ cup batter into hot oiled pan for each pancake. Cook for 2-3 minutes until bubbles appear on the pancake and cooked side is light brown. Turn and cook for 2 more minutes, or until golden. Serve with maple syrup.

Make Ahead: Batter can be made a day ahead and stored in the refrigerator (stir before using). Or pancakes can be frozen after cooking. Cool and store flat in a self-locking plastic bag. Reheat pancakes, covered by a moist paper towel, in a 200° oven.

Microwave: Reheat on high, 20 seconds per pancake; separate and rearrange cakes halfway through cooking.

(cont'd)

Notes: An easy way to grease the pan is to run the end of a stick of butter over the pan's hot surface. Repeat after each panful.

To clean blender easily, put 3 inches of hot water and a squirt of dishwashing detergent in the blender. Cover and turn on high for a minute. Rinse thoroughly.

Fruit Yogurt Pancakes
Prep. 10 min. Cook 6 min. Makes 10.

Use your favorite yogurt in this rich recipe.

1 cup apple yogurt
2 egg yolks
¾ cup flour
1 tablespoon sugar
1 teaspoon baking soda
½ teaspoon salt
½ cup melted butter or margarine
2 egg whites, beaten

Beat yogurt and yolks together. Add sifted dry ingredients. Beat in melted butter. Fold in egg whites which have been beaten to form shiny, soft peaks. Using about half a ladle full of batter for each pancake, cook them in a lightly greased frying pan over medium-high heat. After 3-4 minutes, when bubbles form throughout the cake, turn and cook an additional 2 minutes, or until golden brown. Serve with maple syrup.

Make Ahead: Batter may be stored in the refrigerator for 2-3 days. Leftover pancakes may be cooled and frozen flat in an airtight plastic bag. Reheat them, covered with a moist paper towel, in a 200° oven.

Microwave: Spread out 3 frozen pancakes. Heat on high for 60 seconds.

Note: Blueberry yogurt is a good change from apple, but add 2 drops of blue food coloring if you don't want green pancakes. Banana yogurt makes another good substitute.

Swedish Pancakes
Prep. 5 min. Cook 6 min. Serves 8-10.

The delicate texture makes it easy to eat many of these.

1 cup flour, preferably "instantized" quick-mix variety (like Wondra)
2 tablespoons sugar
¼ teaspoon salt
¼ teaspoon nutmeg
¼ teaspoon cinnamon
3 eggs
3 cups milk
¼ teaspoon vanilla

Sift dry ingredients together in a large bowl. Blend in eggs and milk. Add vanilla. Batter should be the consistency of heavy cream. Cook in a buttered plätt pan* over medium-high heat for 2-4 minutes, then turn to cook other side. Smear butter into each well after every pancake. (Use a sandwich spreader as a small spatula.) Serve with maple syrup.

Make Ahead: Cooked pancakes freeze well in airtight plastic bags for up to 6 months, but be sure to cool them before placing them *flat* in a bag. Frozen pancakes can be reheated on an ovenproof plate, covered with a moist paper towel, in a 200° oven.

Microwave: Place frozen pancakes on a plate or in the *opened* bag in the microwave. For 10 cakes cook on defrost for 5 minutes; separate cakes; heat on high for 3 more minutes.

Note: If using regular flour, let batter stand covered in the refrigerator for at least 2-3 hours or overnight.

*Plätt pan is a frying pan with individual shallow wells 2 inches in diameter. A small frying pan, with a tablespoon of butter at a time, may be used instead, but turning the pancakes is more difficult.

Banana Pancakes
Prep. 5 min. Cook 6 min. Makes eight 5″ pancakes.

A hearty way to start the day. Lovely with bacon.

2 teaspoons lemon juice
¾ to 1 cup milk, depending on desired thickness
1 cup sifted flour
1 teaspoon baking powder
½ teaspoon salt
⅛ teaspoon baking soda
2 tablespoons confectioners sugar
1 egg
½ teaspoon vanilla
1 medium banana, peeled and mashed

Add lemon juice to milk and let stand. Sift together dry ingredients and set aside. In a large bowl combine egg and lemon-milk mixture and beat until foamy. Beat in vanilla and banana. Stir in flour mixture but do not overmix. Batter should be slightly lumpy.

Cook on a hot greased griddle (375°) until tops are bubbly and the edges look dry, about 2 minutes. Turn and brown on the other side. Serve hot with butter and maple syrup.

Make Ahead: Cooked pancakes freeze well if cooled and stored flat in self-sealing plastic bags. Place on a plate, cover with a moist paper towel, and reheat in a 200° oven.

Microwave: Heat on high 20 seconds per frozen pancake. Separate and rearrange cakes halfway through heating.

Note: Rubbing the end of a stick of butter on the hot griddle is an easy way to grease it.

Delicate Corn Cakes
Prep. 5 min. Cook 10 min. Serves 4.

Subtle corn flavor. Serve these anytime.

1 cup flour
2 teaspoons baking powder
½ teaspoon salt
2 teaspoons sugar
2 eggs
1¼ cups milk
1 cup creamed corn, puréed in blender (8.5-ounce can)
½ tablespoon oil for cooking cakes

Sift dry ingredients together into a large bowl. Add eggs and beat well. Beat in milk and corn which has been thoroughly puréed. Heat oil in a frying pan over medium-high heat (375°). Use ¼ cup batter for each pancake. Cook until bubbles appear on the top, about 3 minutes. Turn and cook until other side is golden brown. Serve hot with butter and maple syrup.

Make Ahead: Cooked cakes freeze well if cooled and frozen flat in self-sealing plastic bags. Reheat, covered with a moist paper towel, in a 200° oven. *(cont'd)*

Microwave: Cook on high for 20 seconds per frozen pancake. Separate cakes and rearrange halfway through cooking time.

Buttermilk Puffs

Prep. 15 min. Cook 15 min. Makes 2 dozen.

These taste fresh even if they have been frozen.

6 cups cooking oil, or enough for a
    depth of at least 1½″ in a deep
    frying pan or deep-fat fryer
2 cups sifted flour
¼ cup sugar
1 teaspoon baking powder
½ teaspoon baking soda
½ teaspoon nutmeg or mace
1 teaspoon salt
¾ cup buttermilk
¼ cup vegetable oil
1 egg
Granulated or confectioners sugar

Heat cooking oil in pan or fryer to 375°. Sift dry ingredients into a large bowl. Add buttermilk, ¼ cup oil, and egg. Beat until smooth. Drop tea-spoonfuls of batter into hot oil and fry until golden brown, about 6-8 minutes. Watch and turn puffs to en-sure even cooking on all sides. Drain on paper towel. Roll while still warm in granulated or confectioners sugar.

Make Ahead: Cooled puffs freeze well. Place on cookie sheet in freezer for 30 minutes, then transfer to a plastic bag or airtight container. Serve warm or at room temperature.

Note: To recycle oil for future use, peel and slice in half a small potato. Fry it in oil for 5 minutes to absorb any flavor. Strain oil through a cheese-cloth-lined funnel. Oil will be fine for frying, but not for baking or salad dressing.

Shirred Eggs

Prep. 5 min. Cook 10 min. Serves 1.

One of the nicest things you can do to an egg.

1 thin slice ham
1 to 2 eggs
1 tablespoon butter or margarine
2 tablespoons heavy cream
1 to 2 teaspoons sherry
1 tablespoon grated Swiss cheese

Preheat oven to 350°. Grease a small ovenproof dish or pan. Put ham slice on the bottom and cover with 1 or 2 eggs, being careful not to break the yolks. Cover egg(s) with dots of butter, cream, and sherry. Top with cheese. Bake for 10 minutes for 1 egg, 15 minutes for 2. Whites should be cooked, yolks still runny. Serve in the cooking dish.

Poached Omelet

Prep. 10 min. Cook 15 min. Serves 2.

Light orange taste. Almost like a cus-tard in texture.

2 eggs
½ teaspoon salt
1 teaspoon sugar
1 orange
½ cup milk
1 teaspoon butter or margarine
1 thin slice of orange cut in half (for
    decoration)

Beat eggs until frothy. Add salt

and sugar. Peel orange, reserving the peel. Put milk in saucepan, add peel, and scald milk (heat until bubbles form around edges of pan). Remove peel and add milk in a thin stream to the eggs while beating them. Grease top half of a double boiler with butter or margarine. Add eggs and cover pan. Cook over boiling water for 15 minutes, or until firm. Decorate with orange slice before serving.

French Toast

Prep. 5 min. Cook 10 min. Serves 2.

Easy to make ahead for a popular breakfast.

2 eggs
½ teaspoon vanilla
1 tablespoon confectioners sugar
1 tablespoon light cream or milk
6 slices white bread, trimmed of
  crusts
1 tablespoon butter or margarine
  plus ½ tablespoon oil for frying

With a fork, beat eggs, vanilla, sugar, and light cream together. Dip bread in egg mixture. Cook in greased frying pan over medium-high heat (375°) for 2-3 minutes per side until lightly browned. Serve hot with butter and maple syrup.

Make Ahead: Batter can be made up to two days ahead and refrigerated. Bread can be coated with batter, stacked with waxed paper or foil between the slices, and refrigerated overnight. After cooking, French toast can be cooled, frozen flat, and sealed in a plastic bag. Reheat, covered with a moist paper towel, in a 200° oven.

Microwave: Heat frozen French toast on high for 25 seconds per slice.

Separate and rearrange halfway through cooking.

Jam Toast

Prep. 5 min. Cook 10 min. Makes 12 finger sandwiches.

Attractive side dish for any brunch. Ideal for a buffet.

8 slices white bread
4 tablespoons butter
⅓ cup jam

Trim crust from bread. Spread half the pieces with a generous helping of your favorite jam. Cover with remaining slices to make individual sandwiches. Lightly butter the outside of each sandwich and fry over medium-low heat until lightly browned, about 2 minutes per side. Cut into thin strips or decorative shapes with a cookie cutter. Serve warm.

Luncheon or Supper

Soups and Sandwiches

Light Moussaka Soup

Prep. 20 min. Cook 30 min. Serves 6.

All the taste of moussaka without the calories.

½ pound lean ground lamb
3 cups beef broth
1 tablespoon minced onion
1 small eggplant, peeled and diced
2 stalks celery, without leaves, cut in pieces
1 can (16 ounces) plum tomatoes, undrained
1 clove garlic, minced
1 teaspoon oregano
1 teaspoon basil
2 tablespoons parsley
2 slices white bread
2 tablespoons grated Gruyère cheese

Shape meat into teaspoon-sized balls and broil, turning occasionally, until brown. Drain off any fat. In a large pot bring beef broth to a boil. Add meatballs and other ingredients except bread and cheese. Cover pan and simmer for 30 minutes. Trim crust from bread; cut into circles with 1½″ cookie cutter. Put a round of bread in the bottom of each soup bowl, sprinkle with cheese, and pour hot soup on top.

Vermont Butternut Soup

Prep. 20 min. Cook 45 min. Serves 12.

Maple syrup brings out the best butternut flavor.

3 tablespoons butter or margarine
2 tablespoons chopped onion
1 medium carrot, peeled and chopped
3 tablespoons flour
4 cups warm chicken stock
2 pounds butternut squash, peeled, seeded, and cut in large cubes (about 9 cups)
1 clove garlic
1 tablespoon dried parsley
1½ cups milk
½ cup light cream
2 tablespoons maple syrup or to taste

In a large kettle melt butter and add onion and carrot. Cook over medium-low heat, about 5 minutes, until onions are tender. Sprinkle with flour and continue cooking for 3 minutes while stirring constantly. Remove from heat and blend in warmed chicken stock. Add squash, garlic, and parsley, and simmer covered for 45 minutes. Cool. Purée in batches in blender or food processor. Transfer to kettle, add milk, cream, and syrup, and heat through.

Make Ahead: May be frozen in an airtight container after puréeing but before adding milk, cream, and syrup. If not using full amount of frozen soup, or if planning to freeze some of it, use ½ cup squash purée, 1 teaspoon syrup, 2 tablespoons milk, and 2 teaspoons cream per person.

Easy Carrot Soup

Prep. 35 min. Cook 1 hr. Serves 8-10.

Great for supper. Two methods of preparation make deliciously different soups.

1 pound carrots, peeled and sliced (about 4 cups)
2 medium onions, minced (about ¾ cup)
4 tablespoons butter or margarine
8 cups chicken broth
¼ cup raw rice (not instant)
2 tablespoons tomato paste
½ teaspoon salt
2 teaspoons sugar
Salt and pepper to taste
¾ cup light cream

Sauté carrots and onions in butter over low heat, stirring occasionally, until onions are tender, about 5 minutes. Add all other ingredients except cream. Cover and simmer for 1 hour. Cool in the refrigerator and skim off any fat from the top. Purée in batches in a blender or food processor. Just before serving add cream. Delicious hot or cold.

Make Ahead: May be made a day early and refrigerated or frozen in an airtight container before adding cream.

Variation: For a country texture and fewer calories, omit the cream and do not purée.

Delicious Vegetable Soup

Prep. 20 min. Cook 30 min. Serves 8-10.

Delicious but nonfattening — a dieter's best friend. Superb first course for a luncheon.

2 quarts chicken broth
½ teaspoon dried basil
½ teaspoon dried marjoram
½ teaspoon celery seeds
½ teaspoon dried dill
½ teaspoon dried tarragon
1 clove garlic, minced
1½ cups shredded cabbage
1 cup thinly sliced, peeled carrots
1½ cups fresh green beans (cut in 1-inch pieces)
1½ cups stewed canned tomatoes, undrained
¼ pound sliced fresh mushrooms
¼ cup minced onions
1 cup bean sprouts
Salt and pepper to taste

In a large kettle combine broth and herbs. Bring to a boil over high heat. Add cabbage and carrots. Cover, reduce to low heat, and simmer 15 minutes. Add beans, tomatoes, mushrooms, onions, and bean sprouts. Cover and simmer 10 more minutes, until vegetables are tender. Season to taste.

Sonny's Onion Soup

Prep. 45 min. Cook 30 min. Serves 10-12.

Wine and cognac simmer to a magical flavor and make a fine addition to this old favorite.

3 tablespoons butter or margarine
1 tablespoon vegetable oil
5 cups thinly sliced onions
1 teaspoon salt
¼ teaspoon sugar
3 tablespoons flour

2 quarts boiling beef stock
½ cup dry vermouth
1 cup cognac
1 bay leaf
¼ teaspoon marjoram

Melt butter in a heavy kettle, add oil and onions; cook covered over low heat for 10 minutes. Uncover and raise heat to medium. Stir in salt and sugar, cook for 25 minutes. Stir often until onions are dark brown and reduced to one-fifth of original volume. Sprinkle with flour and cook 3 minutes while stirring frequently. Add boiling stock, wine, cognac, bay leaf, and marjoram. Simmer covered 30 minutes. Remove bay leaf before serving.

Potato Potage

Prep. 30 min. Cook 10 min. Serves 8-10.

A hearty country soup with subtle flavor. We still can't decide whether it tastes better with curry or dill.

5 large red potatoes
1 medium onion, sliced
1 carrot, peeled and sliced
1 tablespoon salt
¼ teaspoon pepper
4 cups water
1 teaspoon curry or ½ teaspoon dill
1 cup white wine
2 cups light cream or milk
5 slices bacon, fried and crumbled

Don't peel potatoes. Scrub and cut them in chunks. Simmer potatoes, onion, carrot, salt, and pepper in water for about 20 minutes, or until potatoes are tender. Drain, reserving 2 cups cooking water. Purée vegetables in batches in a blender or food processor. Put purée in a large saucepan; add 2 cups cooking water, curry or dill, and wine. Simmer 5-10 minutes while stirring. Add cream and heat on low 2-3 minutes while stirring. (Soup can be thinned with more cream.) Serve hot or cold. Garnish with bacon if desired.

Jack's Reuben Sandwich

Prep. 10 min. Cook 6 min. Serves 4.

The Russian Dressing is a special, moist alternative to sauerkraut.

8 slices bread (pumpernickel, or light or dark rye)
12 slices corned beef
6 slices Swiss cheese
6 tablespoons Russian Dressing (see below)
2 tablespoons butter or margarine, softened

For each sandwich put 3 slices of beef and 1½ slices of cheese covered with 1½ tablespoons dressing between two slices of bread. Cheese may be grated if desired. Make 4 sandwiches. Butter the outsides of the bread and sauté over medium-low heat for 2-3 minutes or until bottom slices are lightly browned and cheese is melted. Turn and cook the other sides in a similar manner.

Russian Dressing

½ cup mayonnaise
¼ cup catsup
¼ cup chili sauce
1½ teaspoons minced dill pickle
⅛ teaspoon minced onion
2 tablespoons minced celery
⅛ teaspoon lemon juice
Dash Worcestershire sauce

Mix all ingredients together, blending thoroughly.

Baked Alaska Crab Sandwich

Prep. 15 min. Cook 20 min. Serves 8.

A superb and unusual hot crab delight. Popular with family and guests.

6 ounces crab meat
8 ounces cream cheese
2 tablespoons mayonnaise
½ teaspoon salt
1 teaspoon minced onion
½ teaspoon Worcestershire sauce
4 English muffins, split, toasted, and buttered
2 eggs, separated
2 tablespoons flour
⅓ cup grated Swiss cheese

Preheat oven to 350°. Combine crab meat, cream cheese, mayonnaise, salt, onion, and Worcestershire sauce in blender or food processor. Spread mixture evenly on the eight muffin halves. Beat egg yolks until thick and lemon colored, blend in flour, and stir in Swiss cheese. Beat egg whites until stiff. Fold whites gently into yolk mixture. Spread over muffins and bake for 20 minutes until light brown. Serve immediately.

Make Ahead: Before baking, sandwiches may be frozen on a cookie sheet until hard (30 minutes). Then wrap in foil. Bake frozen, unwrapped, at 350° for 40 minutes.

Microwave: Divide recipe in half. Place 4 halves in a circle. Cook on high for 9 minutes, rotating ¼ turn every 3 minutes.

Cheeses and Quiches

Basic Food Processor Pie Crust Dough

Prep. 5 min. Makes enough for one 9″ or 10″ crust.

Quick, delectable, and foolproof. Excellent for quiches and pies.

1⅓ cups sifted flour
½ cup *cold* butter
½ teaspoon salt
1 tablespoon sugar
2 tablespoons ice water

Put flour, butter cut into 8 pieces, salt, and sugar into bowl of food processor. Use the steel knife and blend for 11 seconds. Keep the machine on and slowly pour water through the feed tube. Run processor for 20 to 50 seconds until dough begins to stick together in clumps. Turn out onto floured board and roll out dough with a rolling pin. Do not double recipe. See individual recipes for baking instructions.

Butter Pie Crust Dough

Prep. 10 min. Makes enough for one 9″ or 10″ crust.

Makes a superior crust in minutes without a food processor. This recipe can be doubled for a two-crust pie.

1⅓ cups sifted flour
1 tablespoon sugar
½ teaspoon salt
½ cup *cold* butter
2 tablespoons ice water

Combine dry ingredients and cut in butter with a pastry knife. Use as few strokes as possible. Lumps of dough should be pea-sized. Mix in water with a fork until dough forms a ball, but isn't sticky. If too sticky, add more flour. (Use less water on a humid day.) Roll out on a floured board with a rolling pin. See individual recipes for baking instructions.

Cheese Velvet

Prep. 10 min. Cook 30 min. Serves 8.

Combines the creamy smoothness of custard with the flavor of a quiche. Cook this luncheon favorite in either the oven or electric frying pan.

4 eggs
2 cups light cream
6 slices bacon, cooked and crumbled
⅛ teaspoon garlic powder
⅛ teaspoon salt
1½ cups grated Gruyère cheese (5 ounces)

Preheat oven to 350°. Beat eggs thoroughly. Gradually add cream while still beating. Add bacon, seasonings, and cheese and mix well. Pour into 8 lightly greased custard cups. Place cups in a shallow pan half filled with hot water. Bake for 30 minutes, or cook at 250° for 30 minutes in a covered electric frying pan that has 1″ water in the bottom.

Make Ahead: Bake for 15 minutes, allow to cool, and cover cups with foil. Place in freezer but keep cups level as custard is still liquid. To serve, bake frozen in a pan of water for 30 minutes at 350°.

Microwave: To cook bacon, place 6 strips of bacon on 3 layers of paper towel. Cover with two more layers of towel. Cook on high for 4 minutes 30 seconds.

Alpine Cheese Fondue
Prep. 5 min. Cook 10 min. Serves 4.

An informal, sociable way to entertain. Less kirsch than usual brings out the wine and cheese flavors.

½ pound Gruyère cheese
½ pound Swiss Emmenthaler cheese
2 tablespoons flour
1 cup dry vermouth
1 teaspoon kirsch
⅛ teaspoon pepper
½ loaf French bread, cubed
2 apples, peeled, cored, and cubed

Coarsely grate cheeses, toss with flour, and set aside. Heat vermouth, kirsch, and pepper in a fondue pot on the stove until almost boiling. Slowly add cheese and stir constantly. When cheese is melted and mixed with wine, transfer pot to fondue flame. Use fondue forks to dip bread and apple in cheese.

Special Quiche Lorraine
Prep. 15 min. Cook 40 min. Serves 6.

The technique for freezing this quiche preserves its special flavor and makes it easy to keep one on hand.

9″ unbaked pie shell (commercially frozen or use recipe on p. 46)
10 slices bacon
6 ounces grated Swiss cheese (1½ cups)
1 tablespoon flour
½ teaspoon salt
¼ teaspoon nutmeg
2 eggs, beaten
1 cup light cream or half-and-half

Preheat oven to 400°. Place a smaller pie plate (greased on bottom) inside the crust and bake for 7 minutes. Remove the inside plate, prick dough with a fork several times, and bake another 5 minutes. Set aside to cool.

Reset oven to 325°. Fry bacon until crisp; drain and crumble. Put half of bacon into pie shell. Mix cheese and flour and sprinkle over bacon. Beat salt, nutmeg, eggs, and cream together and pour over cheese. Top with remaining bacon. Bake for 40 minutes, or until custard is firm and brown. Serve hot or cold.

Make Ahead: If serving cold, bake the day before and refrigerate, as standing improves flavor. To freeze, pour quiche mixture into frozen, partly baked pie shell. Wrap tightly in foil and freeze unbaked on a level shelf. When ready to use, unwrap and bake frozen at 375° for 1 hour.

Crustless Quiche
Prep. 10 min. Cook 30 min. Serves 6.

No crust, no fuss. Crab and artichoke combine with cheese for a rich taste with no dough.

6 ounces crab meat
1 cup canned artichoke hearts or bottoms, packed in water, drained and quartered
2 tablespoons minced onion
2 tablespoons butter or margarine
1 tablespoon oil
1 tablespoon flour

2 cups shredded Monterey Jack
cheese
2 eggs
1 cup light cream
¼ teaspoon Worcestershire sauce
½ teaspoon salt

Preheat oven to 375°. Sauté crab meat, artichokes, and onion in butter and oil over medium heat for 3 minutes. Remove vegetables and meat with a slotted spoon and spread evenly in a greased 9″ pie plate. Sprinkle flour and 1 cup shredded cheese on top. Beat eggs until light and blend with cream, remaining cheese, Worcestershire sauce, and salt. Pour over vegetables. Bake for 30 minutes, or until a thin knife inserted in the center comes out clean.

Microwave: Use a glass pie plate. Cook on high for 2 minutes. Rotate dish ½ turn. Microwave on high for 6 minutes. Rotate dish ½ turn. Cook 5 more minutes. Let stand in oven 7 minutes.

Sherried Turkey Quiche

Prep. 15 min. Cook 40 min. Serves 4-6.

Turns turkey or chicken salad into a freezable sherried custard.

9″ or 10″ unbaked pie shell
3 tablespoons mayonnaise
1 cup diced cooked turkey or chicken
2 eggs
1 teaspoon salt
3 tablespoons dry sherry
⅔ cup milk

Preheat oven to 400°. Use either a commercially frozen crust or the recipe on p. 46. Place a smaller pie plate

(greased on bottom) inside the crust and bake for 7 minutes. Remove the inside plate, prick dough with a fork several times, and bake another 5 minutes. Remove from oven and cool.

In a small bowl mix mayonnaise and meat. Spread on the bottom of the partially baked and cooled pie shell. Reset oven for 350°. Beat eggs until light (about 2 minutes); add salt and sherry, and beat again. Scald milk in saucepan (cook over low heat until bubbles form around edge of pan). Add to egg mixture in a thin stream while continuing to beat. Pour custard over meat. Bake for 40 minutes, or until custard is firm. Serve warm or cold.

Make Ahead: Freeze partly baked pie shell. Pour in quiche mixture, wrap tightly, and freeze unbaked on a level shelf. When ready to use, unwrap and bake frozen at 375° for 1 hour.

Mushroom or Artichoke Tart

Prep. 30 min. Cook 35 min. Serves 4-6.

A vegetable tart which is a welcome change from the usual spinach quiche.

9″ or 10″ pie crust
2 cups artichoke hearts or bottoms, packed in water, **OR** 1½ cups sliced fresh mushrooms, 2 tablespoons butter, and 1 tablespoon oil
2 tablespoons grated Parmesan cheese
¼ cup butter or margarine
2 tablespoons dry white wine
2 eggs
1 teaspoon salt
⅔ cup milk

Preheat oven to 400°. Use either a commercially frozen crust or recipe on p. 46. Bake pie crust with smaller pie plate (greased on bottom) inside the crust for 7 minutes. Remove smaller plate, prick crust with a fork several times, and return to oven for 5 more minutes. Cool.

Reset oven to 350°. Quarter artichokes, drain well, and put in bottom of pie crust, **OR** sauté mushrooms in 2 tablespoons butter and 1 tablespoon cooking oil over medium heat for 5 minutes until lightly browned. Drain and spread in pie crust.

Sprinkle Parmesan cheese on top. Melt butter with wine over low heat and pour over artichokes (or mushrooms) and cheese. Beat eggs well, then beat in salt. Scald milk; pour in a thin stream into eggs while still beating. Do not overbeat so that it foams. Pour into pie crust. Bake for 35-40 minutes.

Make Ahead: Freeze partly baked pie shell. Pour in quiche mixture, wrap tightly, and freeze unbaked on a level shelf. When ready to use, unwrap and bake frozen at 375° for 1 hour.

Salads and Molds

Chicken Salad with Cashews

Prep. 15 min. Serves 8.

Chicken, fruit, and nuts give varied texture and taste to this pretty, refreshing salad.

3-pound chicken, cooked, skinned, boned, cut into bite-sized pieces

1 cup peeled, cored, coarsely chopped apple, tossed in a mixture of 1 tablespoon water and 1 tablespoon lemon juice

¾ cup chopped celery

½ cup cashews

½ cup mayonnaise

¼ teaspoon curry powder

Salt and pepper

Mix meat, fruit, celery, and nuts together. Mix mayonnaise with curry and combine with chicken mixture. Season to taste. Put salad in a ring mold and chill until ready to serve on a bed of lettuce. (Garnish if desired with sliced cherry tomatoes and hard-boiled eggs.)

Single Seafood Salad
Prep. 10 min. Serves 4.

A quick, surefire way to present a very special salad.

1 pound cooked crab meat, shrimp, or lobster

⅔ cup mayonnaise

½ cup catsup

1 tablespoon lemon juice

3 tablespoons dry sherry

⅓ cup diced celery (optional for either shrimp or lobster)

Put seafood in bowl. Mix remaining ingredients together and combine with seafood. Chill until ready to serve on a bed of lettuce. (Garnish if desired with sliced hard-boiled eggs and sliced tomatoes.)

Simple Salmon Mousse
Prep. 5 min. Chill 2 hr. Serves 4.

Smooth, cool, and beautiful for a summer meal.

1 tablespoon plain gelatin
1 tablespoon lemon juice
1 tablespoon chopped onion
1 teaspoon dried dill weed
½ cup boiling chicken stock or
    bouillon
1 can (16 ounces) pink salmon,
    drained, bones and dark meat
    removed
2 drops red food coloring (optional)
½ cup mayonnaise
1 cup medium cream

Put gelatin, lemon juice, onion, and dill in blender or food processor with steel knife. Add boiling stock and blend on high for 30 seconds. Turn off motor. Add salmon, food coloring, and mayonnaise. Blend until well mixed, about 40 seconds. Gradually add cream with motor running. Blend only 30 seconds.

Pour into lightly oiled 4-cup mold or 4 individual cup molds. Chill until firm, about 2-3 hours. To serve, invert mold onto a bed of lettuce. Rub mold with a hot wet towel to loosen mousse.

Make Ahead: May be made a day ahead. Store in covered mold in the refrigerator.

Note: Molds with gelatin do not freeze well.

Variation: For a less expensive dish, substitute for the salmon two 7-ounce cans of tuna packed in water and drained. Omit red food coloring.

Slimming Strawberry Mousse

Prep. 10 min. Chill 4 hr. Serves 8.

A maximum of flavor with a minimum of calories. Nondieters will love it too.

2 tablespoons unflavored gelatin
2 tablespoons water
3 cups fresh strawberries or 16 ounces
    unsweetened frozen strawberries
1 tablespoon sugar
1½ cups unflavored low fat yogurt
1 medium banana, peeled
¼ teaspoon cinnamon
1½ grams noncaloric sweetener or
    equivalent
¼ cup water

Lightly oil a 4-cup mold. Soften gelatin in 2 tablespoons water for 5 minutes. Cut 18 strawberries in half, sprinkle cut side with 1 tablespoon sugar, and set aside. Purée yogurt, remaining strawberries, banana, cinnamon, and sweetener in blender or food processor (use steel knife). Bring ¼ cup water to a full boil and mix in gelatin until completely dissolved. Heat strawberry purée until *hot* to the touch but not boiling and stir in gelatin mixture.

Put half of the sweetened strawberries in the bottom of the mold, cut side up. Pour in half of the yogurt mixture. Add remaining strawberries and top with remaining yogurt mixture. Chill 4 hours or overnight before unmolding.

Note: Leftovers may be *gently* reheated to liquid state, poured into a smaller mold, and re-chilled. This is a handy way to freshen day-old molds.

Avocado Chutney Ring
Prep. 10 min. Chill 4 hr. Serves 4.

Fabulous as a ring mold with crab or chicken salad in the center.

2 tablespoons unflavored gelatin
1 tablespoon lemon juice
1/4 cup good imported chutney
1 large ripe avocado, peeled and pitted
1 tablespoon mayonnaise
2 cups chicken broth

Soften gelatin in lemon juice for 5 minutes. Purée chutney, avocado, and mayonnaise in a blender or food processor (use steel knife). Heat chicken broth to a boil. Dissolve softened gelatin completely in chicken broth. Cool gelatin mixture to room temperature, then blend in avocado purée until smooth and creamy. Pour into lightly oiled 2-cup mold. Chill for 4 hours or overnight before unmolding.

Diet Asparagus Mold
Prep. 10 min. Chill 4 hr. Serves 8.

Designed for the dieter who likes crunch as well as good taste in a salad.

2 tablespoons unflavored gelatin
1/2 cup water
1 1/2 cups diet ginger ale
1/2 teaspoon salt
2 tablespoons fresh lemon juice
1/2 cup finely chopped celery
2 tablespoons grated onion (1 small onion)
1/2 cup coarsely chopped water chestnuts
1 1/2 cups cooked fresh or frozen as-paragus or a 10-ounce can of asparagus, drained and cut into 1" pieces
1/2 cup green seedless grapes

Soften gelatin in water and set aside. Bring ginger ale, salt, and lemon juice to a boil. Add softened gelatin and stir until dissolved. Add celery, onion, chestnuts, and asparagus; stir and heat until warm. Remove from stove. Add grapes. Pour into lightly oiled 1 1/2-quart mold. Refrigerate 4 hours or overnight before unmolding.

Make Ahead: Can be made up to 2 days in advance: store in covered mold in the refrigerator.

Foolproof Tomato Aspic
Prep. 15 min. Chill 3-4 hr. Serves 6-8.

Tarragon brings out the best tomato flavor. Fill the center of the ring with Single Seafood Salad (p. 49) for an extra-special dish.

2 tablespoons plain gelatin
4 cups tomato juice
1/4 teaspoon tarragon
1/4 teaspoon Worcestershire sauce
2 tablespoons dry sherry

Soak gelatin in 1/2 cup tomato juice for 5 minutes. Heat remaining juice, tarragon, Worcestershire sauce, and sherry to almost a boil. Strain into another saucepan. Dissolve softened gelatin in hot juice mixture, then pour into a lightly oiled 4-cup mold and refrigerate until set, about 3-4 hours or more.

Make Ahead: Aspic keeps well for a day in the refrigerator. See note on remolding with Slimming Strawberry Mousse recipe.

Minted Fruit Mold
Prep. 20 min. Chill 3 hr. Serves 4-6.

This light, easy-to-make-ahead salad can be changed to fit your favorite fruit in season.

2 tablespoons unflavored gelatin
1 cup orange juice
1 teaspoon lemon juice
⅛ teaspoon ginger
1 tablespoon sugar
¼ teaspoon dried mint
1 cup diet or regular ginger ale
2 cups fresh fruit (berries, melon balls, peaches — singly or in combina-tion), cut in attractive pieces

Soak gelatin in orange juice for 5 minutes. Then heat with lemon juice, ginger, sugar, and mint in the top of a double boiler until gelatin is dis-solved. Remove from heat and stir in ginger ale. (Strain mixture if you're fussy about mint leaves.) Pour a thin coating of mixture into a lightly oiled 4-cup mold. Arrange some of the fruit decoratively in the gelatin, press-ing the best looking side of the fruit down. Put additional tablespoonfuls of the gelatin mixture over each piece of fruit. Refrigerate until set (about 15 minutes). Mix rest of the fruit into the remaining gelatin mixture and pour into the mold. Chill about 3 hours, or until firmly set. See **Note** (p. 108) for unmolding directions.

Make Ahead: Refrigerated fruit mold keeps well for a day.

Note: Cut fruits like apples, ba-nanas, and peaches just before using so that they don't turn brown.

Meats and Casseroles

Modern Turkey Divan
Prep. 20 min. Cook 15 min. Serves 4.

Exceptionally light cheese sauce with a hint of mustard turns leftover turkey or chicken into a fine meal.

¼ cup butter or margarine
¼ cup flour
1½ cups chicken broth
1½ teaspoons Dijon mustard
¼ teaspoon salt
¼ teaspoon cayenne pepper
¼ cup light cream
1½ cups grated cheddar cheese
2 cups broccoli spears (10 ounces fro-zen, cooked half the time given on package, and well drained)
2 cups cooked turkey

Preheat oven to 425°. Melt butter in a frying pan, add flour, and stir with a whisk until well blended. Cook over low heat for 2 minutes while stirring constantly with a whisk or wooden spoon. Bring broth to a boil and add all at once to flour mix-ture. Stir briskly until thick and smooth. Remove sauce from heat. Season with mustard, salt, and pepper. Mix in cream and 1 cup cheese.

In a small greased casserole, or in 4 individual casserole dishes, layer broccoli, turkey, and sauce. Sprinkle with remaining cheese and bake, un-covered, for 15 minutes.

Make Ahead: Prepare dish so it is ready for baking. Freeze it uncooked in covered casserole. Bake at 425° for

30-35 minutes if frozen, for 15 if thawed. Cooked leftovers can also be frozen.

Better Baked Beans
Prep. 30 min. Cook 45 min. Serves 4.

Serve over rice as a tempting, economical main dish.

4 strips lean bacon cut in pieces
1 clove garlic, crushed, or ⅛ teaspoon dried
½ cup chopped onion
½ cup chopped ham (optional)
1 can (8 ounces) tomato sauce
1 can (20 ounces) red kidney beans, undrained
2 cups cooked white rice

Fry bacon, garlic, and onion over medium-low heat until bacon is crisp. Stir occasionally. Add ham and tomato sauce, cover pan, and simmer for 20 minutes. Stir in undrained beans. Simmer covered for 45 minutes.

Make Ahead: Freeze cooked beans in self-sealing plastic bag. Remove beans from bag and put in top of double boiler; cook covered, stirring occasionally, until warm, about 20 minutes.

Microwave: Cook frozen beans on high for 6 minutes. Stir occasionally.

Dashing Hamburger Casserole
Prep. 20 min. Cook 30 min. Serves 6.

A simple-to-fix, inexpensive meal that children love.

1 medium onion, chopped (⅔ cup)
1 tablespoon oil
1 pound lean hamburger

1 teaspoon garlic salt
6 to 8 ounces medium noodles
1 cup sour cream
2 tablespoons mayonnaise
½ cup chive cottage cheese
1 can (12 ounces) corn, drained
9 ounces grated yellow cheddar cheese
1 can (8 ounces) tomato sauce

Preheat oven to 350°. Sauté onion in oil until limp; add meat and garlic salt; cook over medium-low heat until thoroughly browned, about 5 minutes. Set aside. Meanwhile, cook noodles according to package directions. Drain grease from cooked meat; mix in sour cream and mayonnaise. Drain noodles and mix with cottage cheese. In a lightly buttered 2-quart casserole, layer noodles, meat, corn, cheddar cheese, and tomato sauce. Make 2-3 layers depending on casserole shape. Bake covered for 30 minutes.

Make Ahead: Freeze before baking in covered casserole. Can be frozen for several weeks. Bake frozen at 350° for 50-60 minutes.

Apple Meat Loaf
Prep. 10 min. Cook 1 hr. Serves 4.

This is the best meat loaf we've ever had. Applesauce and sherry create a unique flavor and texture.

2 tablespoons minced onion
1 tablespoon butter or margarine
3 slices firm white bread, trimmed of crusts
1 pound lean ground chuck
1 teaspoon salt
⅛ teaspoon pepper
⅛ teaspoon thyme

1 egg, beaten
1 cup unsweetened applesauce
¼ cup sherry

Preheat oven to 350°. Sauté onion in butter over medium-low heat until tender, about 5 minutes. Remove from heat. Make bread crumbs in blender or food processor. Mix crumbs with onion and combine with meat, seasonings, egg, and applesauce. Pack into 9″ x 5″ loaf pan and bake for 30 minutes. Skim off any excess fat, poke holes in the meat, and spoon sherry over the top. Bake for 30 minutes more.

Make Ahead: Cooked meat loaf can be refrigerated for a day or frozen for a month with no loss in flavor.

Note: Fat will congeal and can be removed with a spoon if meat loaf is stored in refrigerator after cooking.

Meatball Stroganoff

Prep. 30 min. Cook 15 min. Serves 4-6.

Sensational meatballs in a spectacular sauce.

1 egg, lightly beaten
2 tablespoons minced onion
⅛ teaspoon thyme
½ teaspoon salt
⅛ teaspoon black pepper
¼ teaspoon grated lemon rind
1 pound lean hamburger
4 slices firm white bread, trimmed of crusts
2 tablespoons cooking oil plus 1 tablespoon butter
Sauce (see below)

Combine beaten egg, onion, thyme, salt, and pepper. Add lemon rind, meat, and bread which has been made into fine crumbs in a blender or food processor. Mix by hand until thoroughly combined. Roll into 1½″ balls and brown on all sides in hot oil and butter over medium heat for about 15 minutes. Meanwhile, make sauce. Add meatballs and heat through. Makes 27 meatballs.

Sauce

1 tablespoon cornstarch
1 cup condensed beef broth
⅛ teaspoon garlic powder
1 bay leaf
¼ cup dry sherry
1 cup sour cream

Soften cornstarch in 2 tablespoons broth. Boil gently remaining broth, garlic powder, bay leaf, and sherry for 5 minutes. Remove bay leaf and cool mixture slightly. Add softened cornstarch to broth and heat 2-3 minutes. Stir until it starts to thicken. Add sour cream. Warm on low heat and proceed with recipe.

Make Ahead: Meatballs without sauce may be made a day ahead and stored in the refrigerator or frozen. Completed dish may be frozen in an airtight container. Reheat in the top of a double boiler over boiling water.

Precooked Sausage Shish Kebab

Prep. 30 min. Cook 10 min. Serves 4-6.

A nice change from the usual lamb or beef kebabs. Precooking minimizes the uncertainties of charcoal grilling.

1 Polish sausage, sliced into ¾″ pieces
1 tablespoon butter or margarine
2 pounds small zucchini

1 cup barbecue sauce (either commercial or homemade, see p. 86)
1 pound round steak
½ pound fresh mushrooms
1 tablespoon butter or margarine

Cook sausage in 1 tablespoon butter over medium-low heat until browned on all sides and cooked through, about 25 minutes. Meanwhile, trim ends off zucchini, scrub, and cut into ½″ wide slices. Coat with barbecue sauce and broil in oven 3 inches from broiler for about 3 minutes on each side until vegetable is tender but crisp. Coat steak with barbecue sauce and broil 3 minutes a side in the same manner as the zucchini. Cut steak into 1″ squares. Halve mushrooms and sauté in 1 tablespoon butter for 1 minute.

Arrange sausage, zucchini, steak, and mushroom on six 10″ skewers. Store in refrigerator until ready to cook. Brush generously with barbecue sauce. Heat over charcoal grill or under broiler. Turn frequently until hot.

Make Ahead: Skewered meat and vegetables may be stored wrapped in foil for a day in the refrigerator before grilling or broiling.

Breads

Apple Tea Bread
Prep. 25 min. Cook 50 min. Makes 20 slices.

An out-of-the-ordinary fruit bread made with spices and butter.

½ cup butter or margarine
¾ cup sugar
2 eggs
5 tablespoons apple juice or cider
2 teaspoons baking powder
1 teaspoon baking soda
1 teaspoon salt
1 teaspoon cinnamon
½ teaspoon nutmeg
¼ teaspoon ground ginger
2 cups flour
2 cups peeled, cored, and coarsely chopped apples (3 medium)
½ cup coarsely chopped walnuts

Preheat oven to 350°. Cream butter and sugar until fluffy. Add eggs and beat well. Add apple juice. Sift dry ingredients together and add gradually to butter mixture. Blend well. Fold in apples and nuts. Pour batter into greased 1½-quart loaf pan. Bake for 50 minutes or until a toothpick inserted in center comes out clean. Serve warm or cold.

Make Ahead: Bake and cool thoroughly. Wrap tightly in foil and freeze.

Zucchini Bread
Prep. 20 min. Cook 1 hr. Each loaf yields about 18 slices.

A moist, rich bread that gives this humble vegetable gourmet status.

3 eggs
2 cups peeled, grated raw zucchini (4 small)
2 cups sugar
1 cup vegetable oil
1 tablespoon vanilla
3 cups flour
1 teaspoon salt
½ teaspoon cream of tartar
1½ teaspoons baking soda

4 teaspoons cinnamon

1 cup chopped walnuts (optional)

Preheat oven to 350°. Beat eggs until foamy. Add zucchini, sugar, oil, and vanilla to eggs. Beat until well blended. Sift dry ingredients together and add slowly to zucchini mixture. Blend well. Stir in nuts if desired. Pour batter into 2 well-greased 9"x5" loaf pans and bake for 60 minutes or until a toothpick inserted in center comes out clean.

Make Ahead: Cool thoroughly after baking. Wrap tightly in foil and freeze.

Southern Corn Bread

Prep. 15 min. Cook 45 min. Serves 16.

Nutmeg adds zing to this light bread.

½ cup melted butter or margarine

½ cup sugar

1 egg

1 cup yellow cornmeal

1 cup milk

4 teaspoons baking powder

1 teaspoon salt

¼ teaspoon nutmeg

1 cup flour

Preheat oven to 350°. Beat cooled butter with sugar. Blend in egg, cornmeal, and milk. Sift dry ingredients into batter and mix thoroughly. Pour into greased 9" square pan and bake for 45 minutes, or until top is light brown and a toothpick inserted in the center comes out clean.

Make Ahead: Cool thoroughly after baking. Wrap in airtight foil and freeze; defrost and warm before serving. Will keep fresh a day in the refrigerator.

Microwave: Preheat lightly greased glass pan on high for 1 minute. Pour in batter. Bake on high for 6 minutes, rotating pan ½ turn after 3 minutes. Cool for 10 minutes in microwave.

Cranberry Orange Bread

Prep. 30 min. Cook 50 min. Makes 1 loaf.

Orange juice and apple set this apart from the usual cranberry bread.

¾ cup cranberries, washed and halved

2 tablespoons sugar

2 tablespoons vegetable oil

1 cup sugar

1 egg, beaten

1 teaspoon baking powder

½ teaspoon baking soda

½ teaspoon salt

2 cups flour

¾ cup orange juice

⅓ cup unpeeled, cored, chopped red apple (½ medium)

½ cup coarsely chopped walnuts

Preheat oven to 350°. Toss cranberries in 2 tablespoons sugar and set aside. Blend oil and 1 cup sugar together. Beat in egg. Sift dry ingredients together and add to batter alternately with orange juice. Mix until just blended. Gently stir in cranberries, apples, and nuts. Pour into greased 9"x5" pan or comparable-size ring mold. Bake for about 50 minutes, or until a cake tester inserted in the center comes out clean.

Make Ahead: Wrap cooled bread tightly and freeze.

Herbed Popovers
Prep. 10 min. Cook 20 min. Makes 6.

A touch of dill and onion makes a subtle, flavorful addition.

1 cup flour
½ teaspoon salt
1 teaspoon dill seed
1 tablespoon dried minced onion
2 eggs
¾ cup milk
¼ cup melted butter or margarine

Preheat oven to 400°. Sift flour and salt together into a bowl, gently stir in dill and onion. Beat in eggs. Gradually blend in milk and butter. Batter should be smooth, but do not over-beat. Pour batter into 6 well-greased deep muffin pans or custard cups, allowing room for batter to rise. Cook for 20-25 minutes until puffed and browned. Serve immediately.

Variation: For Yorkshire Pudding, preheat an 8″ square pan; put the ¼ cup melted butter or margarine in pan instead of in batter. Add ¼ cup water to batter, then pour in pan. Bake at 400° for 20 minutes; reduce heat to 350° for 15 more minutes. Serves 6.

Banana Bread
Prep. 20 min. Cook 55 min. Each loaf yields 18 slices.

Orange juice and marmalade make this a moist, distinctive bread. Delicious as toast with cream cheese.

½ cup butter or margarine
1 cup sugar
2 eggs
⅓ cup orange juice
1 tablespoon orange marmalade
1⅓ cups mashed ripe bananas (4 medium)
¼ teaspoon salt
½ teaspoon baking soda
1½ teaspoons baking powder
2 cups sifted flour
½ cup chopped walnuts (optional)

Preheat oven to 350°. Cream butter and sugar together until light. Beat in eggs thoroughly, one at a time. Beat in juice, marmalade, and bananas. Sift dry ingredients together and blend into batter. Fold in nuts. Pour batter into greased 9″x5″ loaf pan and bake for 55 minutes, or until cake tester inserted into center comes out clean.

Make Ahead: Cool thoroughly, wrap tightly in foil, and freeze.

Lemon Nut Muffins
Prep. 20 min. Cook 20 min. Makes 18.

Inspired by a cookie, this adds a sweet touch to any main course.

6 tablespoons melted butter
1 cup sugar
3 eggs, beaten
1 cup sour cream
2 teaspoons grated lemon rind (rind of 1 medium lemon)
2 tablespoons lemon juice
2 cups flour
1 teaspoon baking soda
½ teaspoon salt
½ cup chopped walnuts

Preheat oven to 400°. Beat melted butter and sugar until light. Beat in eggs, sour cream, lemon rind, and lemon juice. Sift flour, soda, and salt to-
(cont'd)

gether and stir into batter. Add nuts.
Do not overmix; batter should be
slightly lumpy. Fill greased muffin
pans two-thirds full. Bake for 20
minutes. Muffins are done when cake
tester inserted in center comes out
clean.

Make Ahead: Muffins stay fresh in
the refrigerator for 1-2 days. Or, cool
after baking and freeze in airtight
wrap for several months.

Snacks

Cookies and Brownies

Spicy Chip Cookies

Prep. 10 min. Cook 6 min. Makes 85 two-inch cookies.

An extraordinarily good chip cookie. Children enjoy decorating them — a good way for young ones to learn colors.

1 cup butter or margarine
1 cup brown sugar
1 cup white sugar
2 eggs
2 teaspoons vanilla
1½ tablespoons water
1 teaspoon baking soda
1 teaspoon salt
1 teaspoon cinnamon
½ teaspoon instant coffee granules
2 cups flour
1 package (11.5 ounces) plain chocolate colored sugar coated candies (M&M's)

Preheat oven to 350°. Cream butter and sugars together. Beat in eggs, vanilla, and water. Sift dry ingredients into batter and mix well. Place rounded teaspoonfuls of batter on a greased or Teflon cookie sheet about 3 inches apart. Place 3 candies on top of each cookie without pressing down. Bake on upper shelf of oven for 6-8 minutes, or until cookies are lightly browned but still soft. Let cool for a few minutes before removing from pan.

Make Ahead: Batter can be prepared and stored in refrigerator for a couple of days until convenient to bake. Cooled baked cookies freeze well in an airtight container.

Note: If your oven has uneven heat, turn the cookie sheet around halfway through cooking time to prevent burning.

Peanut Butterscotch Cookies

Prep. 15 min. Cook 8 min. Makes 4 dozen.

Marvelous blend of flavors. A favorite of young and old.

1 package (6 ounces) butterscotch chips
1 cup peanut butter, chunky or smooth
½ cup butter or margarine
½ cup white sugar
½ cup light brown sugar
2 eggs
½ teaspoon salt
½ teaspoon vanilla
1 cup sifted flour
½ teaspoon baking soda

Preheat oven to 350°. In a saucepan melt chips and peanut butter together over low heat, stirring continuously. Set aside. In a large bowl beat butter and sugars until light and fluffy. Add eggs, peanut butter mixture, salt, and vanilla, beating well after each addition. Sift flour, measure it, then re-sift with soda. Add flour gradually to batter and mix well. Put teaspoonfuls of dough 3 inches apart on well-greased cookie sheet. Bake 8-10 minutes until lightly browned on edges. Let sit 5 minutes before removing from cookie sheets with a spatula.

Make Ahead: Cookies stay fresh for a week in a canister. To freeze for several months, cool after baking and store flat in self-sealing plastic bags.

Cashew Cookies

Prep. 15 min. Cook 20 min. Makes 3 dozen.

Buttery, meltaway balls. Hard to stop after eating the first one.

1 cup butter or margarine
1/4 cup confectioners sugar
1 cup ground cashews (6 ounces)
1 teaspoon vanilla
1 1/2 cups sifted flour
3/4 cup confectioners sugar

Preheat oven to 325°. Cream butter and 1/4 cup confectioners sugar together until light and fluffy. Add nuts, vanilla, and flour and mix well. Shape dough into 1" balls and place on a greased cookie sheet. Bake for 20-25 minutes until bottoms are tan. Shake warm cookies in a bag containing 3/4 cup confectioners sugar. Place on a rack to cool and strain remaining sugar over them.

Make Ahead: Cookies stay fresh for a week in a canister. To freeze, place in a single layer on a cookie sheet and freeze until hard — about 30 minutes. Then transfer to an airtight container and freeze for up to 6 months.

Rum Pecan Puffs

Prep. 15 min. Cook 18 min. Makes

24 cookies.

An easy to make, sophisticated holiday treat.

1/2 cup butter or margarine
1/2 cup confectioners sugar
2 tablespoons dark rum
1 cup pecans
1 cup less 1 tablespoon sifted flour
Confectioners sugar for coating

Preheat oven to 350°. Cream butter and 1/2 cup confectioners sugar together until light. Blend in rum. Grind nuts in blender until fine. Stir pecans and flour into butter mixture. Shape dough into 1" balls. Bake on lightly greased cookie sheet until cookies are firm and bottoms are tan — about 18 minutes. Roll in confectioners sugar while warm.

Make Ahead: Cookies stay fresh in a canister for about a week. To freeze, place in a single layer on a cookie sheet for about 30 minutes and then transfer to an airtight container or self-sealing plastic bag. May be frozen for up to 6 months.

Lemon Meringue Squares

Prep. 20 min. Cook 30 min. Makes 16 squares.

Rich lemony-sweet flavor. Ideal dessert for a buffet, potluck supper, or bake sale.

1/2 cup butter or margarine
1/4 cup white sugar
1/4 cup confectioners sugar
2 egg yolks
1 teaspoon vanilla
1 cup flour
1 teaspoon baking powder

½ teaspoon salt
½ cup coconut
2 egg whites, at room temperature
¼ teaspoon cream of tartar
1 cup white sugar
1 teaspoon grated lemon rind
4 tablespoons lemon juice

Preheat oven to 325°. Cream butter with ¼ cup white sugar and ¼ cup confectioners sugar. Beat in egg yolks and vanilla. Sift flour, baking powder, and salt into batter and beat well. Stir in coconut. Spread crust mixture evenly in a greased 8″ square pan and set aside.

In a bowl, beat egg whites until soft peaks form. Beat in cream of tartar. Gradually add 1 cup white sugar, 2 tablespoons at a time, beating continuously. Beat until whites are stiff and form peaks. Stir in lemon rind and juice. Spread meringue over crust. Bake for 30 minutes until meringue is lightly browned. Let cool for 10 minutes before cutting into squares.

Microwave: Use a glass pan. Cook on high for 6 minutes, rotating ¼ turn every 2 minutes. Let rest 5 minutes in oven.

Make Ahead: Squares stay fresh in the refrigerator for 3 days. Some taste and texture are lost by freezing but it can be done. Place cooled squares on tray and freeze until hard — about 30 minutes. Then store in airtight bags in freezer.

Brandied Pecan Mini-Tarts

Prep. 40 min. Cook 23 min. Makes 30.

Festive appearance, neat to eat, easy to freeze.

Basic Food Processor Pie Crust
    Dough (p. 46), or Butter Pie Crust
    Dough (p. 46), or defrost and use
    your favorite commercially frozen
    dough
2 large eggs
½ cup light brown sugar
2 tablespoons melted butter
1 tablespoon cognac
¾ cup coarsely chopped pecans

Roll dough to ⅛″ thickness and cut it with a fluted 3″ cookie cutter. Fit the 30 cutouts gently into greased 1¾″ tartlet pans.

Preheat oven to 300°. Beat eggs until light. Blend in sugar, butter, and cognac. Stir in pecans. Put a heaping teaspoonful of filling into each mini-tart. Each well should be two-thirds full. Bake for 8 minutes. Raise heat to 375° and bake for 15 more minutes. Cool before removing from pan.

Make Ahead: Cool, freeze on tray, and store in airtight bags in freezer.

Frosted Oatmeal Cookies

Prep. 30 min. Chill 1 hr. Cook 10 min. Makes about 5 dozen.

Dough can be made well ahead; then just slice, bake, and frost. Enjoy the mild coffee-cinnamon flavor.

1 cup butter or margarine
1 cup light brown sugar
1 cup white sugar
2 eggs
2 teaspoons vanilla
1½ cups sifted flour

1 teaspoon baking soda
1 teaspoon cinnamon
1 teaspoon salt
3 cups quick-cooking oatmeal
1 cup coarsely chopped walnuts
Frosting (see below)

Cream butter and sugars together until fluffy. Beat in eggs and then vanilla. Sift flour, soda, cinnamon, and salt together into batter while beating continuously. Stir in oatmeal and nuts. Form into a long roll about 1½″ in diameter and chill for at least an hour. Slice and bake in 350° oven for about 10 minutes.

Frosting

3 tablespoons butter or margarine
1 cup confectioners sugar
1 tablespoon instant coffee granules, crushed or sifted
1 teaspoon vanilla
½ teaspoon cinnamon

Cream butter and sugar together until fluffy. Beat in coffee, vanilla, and cinnamon. Spread on cooled cookies.

Make Ahead: Freeze in a single layer on a tray until frosting is firm — about 30 minutes. Store in airtight container in freezer.

Chocolate Hip Huggers

Prep. 20 min. Cook 12 min. Makes 4 dozen.

These moist, double-chocolate treats are a fine way to satisfy the pangs of a "snack attack."

4 squares (4 ounces) unsweetened chocolate
¾ cup butter or margarine

1¼ cups sugar
3 eggs, separated
1 whole egg
¾ cup flour
¾ teaspoon baking soda
½ teaspoon salt
¼ teaspoon cream of tartar
Dash of salt
⅓ cup sugar
6 ounces semi-sweet chocolate chips (optional)

Preheat oven to 325°. Melt chocolate squares in top of double boiler or microwave. Set aside and cool slightly.

Cream together butter and 1¼ cups sugar and beat until light. Blend in the 3 egg yolks, 1 whole egg, and unsweetened chocolate. Sift flour, soda, and ½ teaspoon salt into batter while beating. Blend well and set aside.

In a separate bowl beat 3 egg whites until foamy. Beat in cream of tartar and dash of salt. Continue beating until soft peaks form. *Gradually* beat in ⅓ cup sugar. Beat until whites are glossy and stiff peaks form. Fold meringue into chocolate mixture. Gently stir in chocolate bits, if desired.

Place heaping teaspoonfuls of batter 2 inches apart on well-greased and floured cookie sheet. Bake for 12-15 minutes. *Do not overcook.* Cookies should be soft and show an imprint if touched. Let cookies harden slightly before removing with a spatula.

Make Ahead: Cool cookies thoroughly before stacking in a canister. To freeze, seal in a single layer in airtight wrap and put in freezer.

Note: To melt chocolate in microwave, unwrap top but leave paper around the bottom and sides of the squares. Cook on high for 2 minutes and 20 seconds.

Sociable Hermits
Prep. 10 min. Chill 1-2 hrs. Cook 8 min. Makes 60.

Baking time is critical to these spicy, chewy delights filled with raisins and nuts.

½ cup butter or margarine
2 cups light brown sugar
2 eggs, beaten
1 tablespoon bourbon
3 cups flour
1 teaspoon baking soda
½ teaspoon salt
½ teaspoon ginger
1 teaspoon cinnamon
⅛ teaspoon ground cloves
2 cups seedless raisins (9-ounce box)
1 cup chopped walnuts

Cream butter and sugar. Beat in eggs and bourbon. Sift together dry ingredients and add to creamed mixture. Dough is stiff at this point, so beat with a dough hook if you have one. Stir in raisins and nuts. Roll dough into a 1½″ diameter cylinder, wrap in wax paper, and chill in refrigerator 1-2 hours. Cut in thin slices. Bake at 350° for 8-10 minutes on a lightly greased cookie sheet. *Do not overbake.* They harden as they cool.

Make Ahead: Freeze cooled baked cookies in airtight wrap.

Creamy Orange Cookies
Prep. 15 min. Cook 8 min. Makes 4 dozen.

Sour cream, citrus, and frosting give these cookies a special lift.

½ cup soft margarine
1½ cups sugar
2 eggs
3 tablespoons orange juice
1 teaspoon grated lemon rind
1 cup sour cream
2¾ cups sifted flour
½ teaspoon baking soda
½ teaspoon salt
Frosting (see below)

Preheat oven to 375°. Cream margarine and sugar together until light. Beat in eggs. Blend in juice, rind, and sour cream. Sift flour, soda, and salt together into batter. Mix well. Drop heaping teaspoonfuls of dough 2 inches apart on a lightly greased cookie sheet. Bake for 8-10 minutes. Cookies should still be white when done, but firm to the touch and light brown underneath. Cool.

Frosting

4 tablespoons melted butter
2 tablespoons orange juice
½ teaspoon lemon rind
½ teaspoon vanilla
1 cup sifted confectioners sugar

Mix melted butter, juice, and rind together. Stir in vanilla and sugar and spread over cooled cookies. Let icing harden on cookies.

Make Ahead: Spread iced cookies on cookie sheet and freeze until firm — at least 30 minutes. Pack loosely in plastic bags and seal tightly.

Blueberry Bars

Prep. 20 min. Cook 40 min. Makes 2 dozen.

Crunchy bottom and moist fruit filling make these an unusual alternative to brownies.

1¾ cups flour
1½ cups light brown sugar
½ cup margarine, cut into 8 pieces
1½ cups finely chopped walnuts
1 cup blueberry yogurt
½ teaspoon cinnamon
1 egg, beaten
2 cups blueberries, fresh or frozen

Preheat oven to 350°. Blend flour, sugar, and margarine together at low speed until fine crumbs form. Stir in nuts. Press 2½ cups of the mixture in ungreased 11″x7″ pan and bake for 10 minutes. Meanwhile, mix remaining crumb mixture with yogurt, cinnamon, and beaten egg. Add blueberries and spread over baked crumb base. Bake for 40-50 minutes, until top is firm. Bars will harden as they cool. Cool and then cut into bars.

Make Ahead: Spread bars in single layer on cookie sheet and freeze until firm. Then seal in airtight wrap and store in freezer.

Helen's Heavenly Nutmeats

Prep. 10 min. Cook 30 min. Makes 4 cups of nut clusters.

Special Christmastime treat from Sweden. Meringue-coated nuts make a lovely gift or party fare.

1½ cups blanched whole almonds (½ pound)
2 cups walnut quarters (½ pound)
2 egg whites, at room temperature
Dash of salt
1 cup fine granulated sugar
½ cup butter or margarine

Toast almonds and walnuts in 300° oven until light brown — about 8 minutes. After five minutes start watching carefully so nuts don't burn. Remove from oven and cool. Reset oven to 325°.

Beat egg whites until soft peaks form. Add salt and gradually beat in sugar, 2 tablespoons at a time. Keep beating until stiff peaks form. Coat nuts with meringue.

Melt butter in a 15″x10″ pan and spread meringue mixture over butter. Bake for about 30 minutes, stirring mixture gently every 10 minutes. Nuts are done when coating turns brown and no butter is left in the pan.

Make Ahead: Store nut clusters at room temperature in canister for a week.

Blond Brownies

Prep. 15 min. Cook 35 min. Makes about 3½ dozen.

Brown sugar and chocolate chips are an irresistible combination.

⅔ cup melted butter or margarine
2¼ cups light brown sugar
3 eggs
2 teaspoons vanilla
2 cups presifted flour
2 teaspoons baking powder
1 teaspoon salt
⅛ teaspoon instant coffee granules,

crushed or sifted

6 ounces semi-sweet chocolate chips

Preheat oven to 325°. Grease a 15"x10" baking pan. Beat melted butter and sugar together. Add eggs, one at a time, beating for a minute after each addition. Blend in vanilla. Sift dry ingredients together and beat well into sugar-egg mixture. Stir in chocolate chips. Pour batter into greased pan. Bake for 35-40 minutes. *Do not overbake.* Brownies should be soft and light brown around the edges.

Make Ahead: Brownies keep in airtight container for a week or freeze well in airtight wrap.

Microwave: Use greased 8" square glass pan. Cook 10 minutes on high. Rotate pan ¼ turn every 3 minutes 20 seconds. Makes 16 thick cake-like brownies.

Fudge Brownies

Prep. 20 min. Cook 25 min. Makes 16.

Moist, rich chocolate with a light interior. Almost as quick as a mix and much better tasting.

½ cup butter or margarine

1 cup sugar

2 eggs

2 ounces (2 squares) unsweetened chocolate, melted and cooled

1 teaspoon vanilla

½ cup sifted flour

1 egg white, at room temperature

⅛ teaspoon salt

2 tablespoons sugar

16 pecans (optional)

Preheat oven to 325°. Cream margarine and 1 cup sugar together until light. Beat in whole eggs, one at a time. Blend in chocolate and vanilla. Slowly add flour.

In a separate bowl, beat egg white until soft peaks form. Beat in salt and two tablespoons sugar. Beat until stiff peaks form. Fold meringue into chocolate mixture. Pour batter into a greased 9" square foil-lined pan. If desired, arrange pecans on top. Bake for 25 minutes. Brownies will be soft but will harden as they cool.

Make Ahead: Cool baked brownies, then freeze flat on a tray until firm. Stack in airtight wrap in the freezer for up to 6 months.

Microwave: Line an 8" square glass pan with wax paper; grease paper and pan sides well. Cook brownie batter on high for 6 minutes, rotating ¼ turn every 2 minutes. Let rest in oven 3 minutes after cooking.

Chocolate Mint Meringues

Prep. 10 min. Cook 20 min. Makes about 3 dozen.

Magically flavored meringue morsels.

2 egg whites, at room temperature

½ teaspoon cream of tartar

¾ cup fine granulated sugar

4 tablespoons unsweetened cocoa

¼ teaspoon pure peppermint extract

6 ounces semi-sweet chocolate chips

Preheat oven to 300°. Beat egg whites until soft peaks form. Add cream of tartar. Continue beating and gradually beat in sugar. When mixture stands in stiff peaks, beat in cocoa and peppermint. Gently fold in chocolate chips. Drop meringue by teaspoonfuls onto lightly greased or nonstick cookie sheets. Bake for 20-25 minutes.

Make Ahead: Store in canister at room temperature for up to a week. Or freeze flat on tray until hard, and then store in airtight wrap in freezer.

Mocha Meringues

Prep. 10 min. Cook 20 min. Makes 3 dozen.

A flavor variation of chocolate mint meringues.

2 egg whites, at room temperature
½ teaspoon cream of tartar
¾ cup fine granulated sugar
¼ teaspoon instant coffee granules, crushed or sifted
2 tablespoons unsweetened cocoa
1 teaspoon vanilla
6 ounces semi-sweet chocolate chips

Preheat oven to 300°. Beat egg whites until soft peaks form. Add cream of tartar. Then beat, gradually adding sugar, until whites stand in stiff glossy peaks when beater is withdrawn. Fold in coffee, cocoa, and vanilla. Stir in chocolate chips. Drop by teaspoonfuls onto lightly greased or nonstick cookie sheets. Bake for about 20-25 minutes.

Make Ahead: Store in canister at room temperature for up to a week. Or freeze flat until hard, and then store in airtight wrap in freezer.

Cocktails

Hot Appetizers

Jamaican Bacon

Prep. 15 min. Cook 15 min. Makes 32-40 hors d'oeuvres.

A favorite of all our guests. Bacon balances the pineapple-rum flavor.

1 can (4 ounces) pineapple slices in unsweetened juice (4-5 slices)
2 tablespoons rum, light or dark
½ pound lean, sliced bacon
2 tablespoons brown sugar, light or dark

Drain pineapple and cut each slice in eight wedges. Mix pineapple and rum together in bowl. Cut bacon slices into thirds. Wrap each third around a pineapple wedge and secure with a toothpick. Arrange in oven-proof pan and sprinkle sugar on top. Cook in 450° oven for 10-15 minutes until bacon is light brown. Drain off fat. Serve warm.

Make Ahead: Recipe can be prepared early in the week, refrigerated, and then cooked when desired. Or before cooking, freeze in airtight wrap and store in freezer for up to a month. Defrost and bake at 450° for 10-15 minutes.

Microwave: Bake only half the recipe at a time: sprinkle sugar on pineapple. Arrange in an 8″ square glass pan or 9″ pie pan.Cover loosely with wax paper. Cook on high for 8 minutes. Rotate ¼ turn every 2 minutes. Let rest 1 minute in oven after cooking. Remaining pineapple pieces in rum can be stored for up to 5-7 days.

Note: For extra flavor, let the pineapple marinate in the rum for an hour or more before wrapping it in bacon.

Clams Casino

Prep. 15 min. Cook 5 min. Makes 18 hors d'oeuvres.

Quick, easy, and distinctive.

1 cup canned clams (8 ounces), or 18 medium quahogs
9 slices bacon
4 tablespoons butter
1 medium onion, minced
⅛ teaspoon garlic powder
1 cup seasoned bread crumbs

Drain canned clams or wash fresh clams well. Let fresh clams soak in cold water and discard any that float. Steam clams open by boiling in water, covered, for 10 minutes. Remove clams from shells but be careful to discard any clams that do not open.

Mince clams in blender or food processor (use steel knife) and set aside. Cook bacon until just barely brown, slightly undercooked. Drain, chop, and reserve.

In a frying pan, melt butter and cook onion and garlic over medium heat until onion is transparent, about 5 minutes. Remove from heat and mix in bread crumbs. Combine crumb mixture, clams, and bacon. Put in clam shells or in pan and bake at 400° for 5 minutes. Serve in clam shells or on crackers.

Gruyère Cubes

Prep. 30 min. Cook 8 min. Makes 3 dozen.

Light cheese puffs that melt in your mouth.

½ cup butter or margarine
1 cup grated Gruyère cheese (4 ounces)
1½ ounces cream cheese
¼ cup milk
Pinch of nutmeg
2 drops Tabasco
2 egg whites
¼ teaspoon cream of tartar
½ pound soft, fresh white bread, unsliced

Melt butter and cheeses with milk in top of double boiler over gently boiling water. Mix well, season with nutmeg and Tabasco, and set aside. Beat egg whites until foamy; add cream of tartar and continue beating until stiff peaks form. Fold whites gently into cheese mixture.

Trim crust from bread, cut the loaf into 1″ cubes, and coat all sides with batter. Place cubes slightly apart on nonstick cookie sheet. Bake at 350° for 4 minutes, until lightly browned on the bottom. Turn cubes and cook for 4 more minutes. Serve warm.

Make Ahead: Dip bread cubes in batter, but do not bake. Place cubes apart on cookie sheet and freeze until solid, about 20 minutes. Store in airtight wrap in freezer. Bake frozen at 400° for 12-15 minutes.

Zucchini Figures

Prep. 15 min. Cook 25 min. Makes 4 dozen hors d'oeuvres.

Fun to make in a variety of shapes.

4 eggs, well beaten
1 cup buttermilk baking mix (like Bisquick)
½ cup grated Swiss cheese
2 tablespoons parsley flakes
⅛ teaspoon dried tarragon
¼ cup minced onion
½ cup milk
3 cups grated, unpeeled zucchini
½ teaspoon salt

Preheat oven to 350°. Combine all ingredients and blend well. Pour batter into 2 greased 8″ square pans. Bake for 25-30 minutes until golden. Cool and cut into squares or desired shapes with small cookie cutters. Serve warm.

Make Ahead: Freeze cooked and cooled figures on cookie sheets until firm. Wrap and store in freezer. Defrost and warm at 300° for 10 minutes. Or make figures up to two days ahead, cover, and refrigerate.

Crab Puffs

Prep. 25 min. Cook 12 min. Makes 6 dozen hors d'oeuvres.

A miniature version of the Baked Alaska Crab Sandwich. Perfect for a fancy cocktail party.

72 toast rounds (18 slices white bread)
6 ounces crab meat
8 ounces cream cheese
2 tablespoons mayonnaise
½ teaspoon salt
½ teaspoon Worcestershire sauce
½ teaspoon lemon juice
1 teaspoon minced onion
2 eggs, separated
2 tablespoons flour
⅓ cup finely grated Swiss cheese

Buy Melba rounds or make your own toast by using a 1½″ cookie cutter or glass to cut rounds from 18 slices firm white bread. Spread rounds on baking sheet and broil until lightly browned (about a minute). Turn and brown other side (about 20 seconds). Watch carefully. These freeze well for later use.

Preheat oven to 350°. Combine crab, cream cheese, mayonnaise, salt, Worcestershire sauce, lemon juice, and onion in blender or food processor (use steel blade) until smooth. Mound crab mixture liberally on rounds and refrigerate while preparing egg mixture.

Beat egg whites until stiff peaks form. Set aside. In a small bowl, beat yolks until lemon colored. Beat in flour. Stir in Swiss cheese. Fold egg whites into yolk mixture. Coat crab mounds with a thin layer of egg. Bake at 350° for 12-15 minutes, until light brown.

Make Ahead: Place rounds with layers of crab and egg on cookie sheet and freeze until firm (about 30 minutes). Store in airtight package in freezer. Bake frozen at 350° for 15-20 minutes.

Microwave: Place 6 frozen puffs in a circle on a plate. Heat on high for 1 minute 30 seconds. Rotate ¼ turn every 30 seconds.

Bacon Crisps

Prep. 10 min. Cook 30 min. Makes 50 hors d'oeuvres.

Simple and good.

10 ounces unsalted crackers (like stone-ground wheat crackers)
½ pound sliced lean bacon, preferably maple flavored or hickory smoked

Cut each cracker into large bite-sized pieces. Wrap a single layer of bacon completely around the cracker, overlapping ends slightly to allow for shrinkage. Bake at 325° for 30 minutes. Serve warm.

Make Ahead: Cooked bacon crisps remain fresh for a day in refrigerator.

Chutney Cheese Canapés

Prep. 10 min. Cook 5 min. Makes 40 canapés.

Very easy, very good, and deceptively elegant.

10 thin slices white bread
3 tablespoons butter
4 ounces chutney (½ cup)
8 ounces grated sharp cheddar cheese (1 cup)
Bacon bits

Use a 1½″ cookie cutter or glass to cut rounds or other desired shapes from bread. Spread rounds on baking sheet and broil until lightly browned (about a minute). Turn and brown other side (about 20 seconds). Watch carefully. (May be frozen at this point for later use.) Spread butter on one side of the toasted rounds.

Preheat oven to 350°. Blend chutney and cheese until smooth in blender or food processor (use steel knife). Spread cheese mixture on buttered side of toast; garnish with bacon bits. Heat about 5 minutes.

Make Ahead: Freeze uncooked canapés on a cookie sheet until firm (about 30 minutes). Transfer to an airtight package in freezer. Bake frozen canapés at 425° for 10 minutes.

Crab Dip

Prep. 10 min. Cook 20 min. Makes about 1 cup.

Keeps well on a hot tray for several hours.

6 ounces cream cheese
¼ cup mayonnaise
1 tablespoon minced onion
¼ teaspoon paprika
½ teaspoon salt
⅛ teaspoon Worcestershire sauce
6 ounces crab meat, fresh, frozen, or canned (and drained)

Preheat oven to 350°. Beat all ingredients together until well mixed. Put in small ovenproof dish. Bake uncovered for 20 minutes. Serve warm with thin unsalted crackers.

Make Ahead: Mix all ingredients, cover, and refrigerate for a day. Bake uncovered at 350° for 20 minutes when ready to use.

Microwave: In 4½″x4½″x2″ ceramic ovenproof dish, loosely covered with wax paper, cook on high for 6 minutes. Rotate ¼ turn every 2 minutes.

Clam Dip

Prep. 10 min. Cook 30 min. Makes 1½ cups.

Equally tasty, but different if mixed by hand or puréed in a processor. Vermouth and cheese complement the clams.

1 can (7 ounces) clams, minced (undrained)
4 tablespoons melted butter or margarine
15 Bremner Wafers, crushed
2 tablespoons seasoned stuffing mix, crushed
⅛ teaspoon garlic powder
2 tablespoons dry vermouth
2 tablespoons grated Gruyère cheese

Preheat oven to 350°. Stir together all but grated cheese. Put in small greased ovenproof casserole and sprinkle with cheese. Bake for 30 minutes. Serve hot with crackers.

Make Ahead: Ingredients can be mixed and refrigerated hours before needed. Bake just before using.

Miniature Quiches

Prep. 30 min. Cook 15 min. Makes 60.

A mini-variety of Special Quiche Lorraine. Wonderful to make ahead for a special party or to keep in reserve for unexpected guests.

Pastry for 2 unbaked 9″ pie shells (commercially frozen or double recipe on p. 46)
1½ cups grated Swiss cheese
1 tablespoon flour
½ teaspoon salt
¼ teaspoon nutmeg
2 eggs, beaten

1 cup milk or light cream
½ cup bacon bits (optional)

Preheat oven to 400°. Roll out pastry dough to ⅛″ thickness on a floured board, cut into 3″ rounds, and fit into greased small tartlet wells. Prick bottom of pastry with a fork. Place another tartlet pan with greased bottom on top of first pan, or grease wax paper and fill paper-lined wells with dried beans, popcorn kernels, etc. to keep pastry from puffing up. Bake for 8 minutes. Remove weights and bake 3-4 minutes more, until pastry is light brown. Cool, run a knife along outside of pastry, remove from pan, and freeze hard.

Reset oven to 350°. See Special Quiche Lorraine recipe (p. 47) for more detailed directions. Fill each frozen tartlet with a little Swiss cheese. Pour well-beaten mixture of flour, salt, nutmeg, eggs, and milk over cheese. Garnish with bacon bits if desired. Bake for 8 minutes.

Make Ahead: Freeze tartlets until custard is solid. Transfer to airtight bags in freezer. Bake frozen at 350° for 15 minutes.

Potato Crisps

Prep. 5 min. Cook 8 min. Serves 4.

Elevates the lowly potato skin to a delectable treat.

¾ cup potato peels (skin from 4 scrubbed medium potatoes)
¾ cup oil
Salt

Cook potato peels in oil that has been heated to 375° in frying pan or deep-fat fryer. (If using fryer, pour oil to depth of 2-3 inches.) Keep pan covered to avoid splattering, stir occasionally, and cook for 8 minutes until peels are crisp. Drain and salt.

Impulse Cheese Dip

Prep. 5 min. Bake 15 min. Serves 6-10.

An exotic party dish that comes from the simplest of ingredients.

10-ounce bar sharp cheddar cheese
1 small onion, minced
¾ cup mayonnaise

Place cheese in small ovenproof casserole. Mix onion and mayonnaise and spread over and around cheese. Bake at 400° for 15 minutes. Serve immediately with crackers.

Make Ahead: Assemble ingredients and refrigerate a day ahead. Bake just before serving.

Microwave: Cook 3 minutes on high. Rotate ¼ turn after each minute.

Cheese Fingers

Prep. 10 min. Cook 10 min. Makes 32-35 fingers.

An easy adaptation of a caterer's specialty. A make-ahead delight.

8 thick slices white bread
1 cup mayonnaise
1 cup fresh, finely grated Parmesan
    cheese (5 ounces)

Preheat oven to 350°. Trim crusts off bread. Cut each slice of bread into 4 or 5 strips. Coat each strip with mayonnaise and roll in cheese. Bake at 350° for 10 minutes or until golden brown.

Make Ahead: Before baking, freeze cheese-coated strips on a cookie sheet for 30 minutes, or until hard. Transfer to an airtight plastic bag and freeze for up to 4 months. Bake frozen at 350° for 12-15 minutes.

Mushroom Rounds

Prep. 20 min. Cook 10 min. Makes 40 canapés.

Cognac adds a touch of class.

8 large mushrooms
4 tablespoons butter or margarine
3 tablespoons finely chopped onion
1½ slices white bread (⅔ cup fresh
    bread crumbs)
¼ teaspoon salt
¼ cup brandy, warmed
10 slices firm white bread

Preheat oven to 425°. Wash and dry mushrooms. Chop finely. Melt butter in frying pan. Sauté onions and mushrooms until limp, about 4 minutes on medium-low heat. Crumb 1½ slices of bread in food processor or blender. Add crumbs and salt to pan and cook for 2 minutes on medium heat. Pour warm brandy into pan and ignite carefully, using long-handled match or kitchen match held by tongs. Cool mushroom mixture while making bread rounds.

Cut 1″ rounds of bread from the 10 slices using a cookie cutter or glass. Spread the rounds with mushroom mixture. Bake on a cookie sheet for 10 minutes.

Make Ahead: Freeze bread rounds, then spread with mushroom mixture. Freeze flat in single layer until hard. Store in airtight wrap in freezer. Bake frozen at 425° for 12 minutes.

Cold Appetizers

Shrimp Cocktail Mousse

Prep. 35 min. Chill 4 hrs. Makes 5 cups.

An exceptionally pretty mold that will serve a crowd. Subtle blend of tomato and shrimp makes it popular.

2 envelopes unflavored gelatin
½ cup cold water
8 ounces cream cheese
1 can (10¾ ounces) tomato soup
1 cup mayonnaise
½ cup minced onion
5 tablespoons chili sauce
1 teaspoon horseradish
2 cans (6 ounces each) small, cleaned shrimp, drained and chopped coarsely

Soften gelatin in cold water for 5 minutes. Cut cream cheese into small pieces. Heat undiluted soup to boiling point over medium-low heat while stirring constantly. Remove from heat. Quickly beat cheese into hot soup. Add gelatin while mixture is still warm and stir until gelatin is thoroughly dissolved. Mix in all other ingredients in order listed. Pour into well-oiled 5-cup metal mold. Fill mold to the top. Chill 4 hours or longer.

To unmold, run knife around perimeter of mold. Hold mold in hot water for 20 seconds, top with serving platter, and quickly invert mold onto platter. If necessary, cover inverted metal mold with hot towels to further loosen mousse. Shaking mold from side to side helps also. Decorate mousse with mayonnaise or parsley if desired. Serve on crackers.

Make Ahead: Shrimp mousse stays fresh for a day in refrigerator. Leftovers can be heated, remolded, and refrigerated for the following day.

Caviar Mold

Prep. 15 min. Chill 4 hrs. Makes 2½ cups.

An inexpensive way to serve an impressive mousse.

1½ envelopes unflavored gelatin
1 tablespoon cold water
¼ cup boiling water
½ teaspoon Worcestershire sauce
1 teaspoon lemon juice
1 tablespoon minced onion
1 cup sour cream
1 cup mayonnaise
4 ounces red caviar
2 hard-boiled eggs, finely chopped

Soften gelatin in cold water for 5 minutes. Dissolve gelatin in ¼ cup boiling water. Stir in Worcestershire sauce, lemon juice, and onion. Cool slightly and add sour cream, mayonnaise, caviar, and eggs. (Reserve a teaspoonful of caviar to decorate mold if desired.) Fill a well-greased 2½-cup metal mold with caviar mixture. Chill for 4 hours or longer. (See previous recipe for unmolding directions.) Serve with crackers.

Make Ahead: Mousse can be made a day in advance and refrigerated. Leftovers can be heated and remolded for the following day.

Party Artichokes and Shrimp

Prep. 40 min. Makes about 40 hors d'oeuvres.

Simple and spectacular. Make early in the day, cover, and refrigerate until ready to use.

1 large artichoke
1 can (6 ounces) small cleaned shrimp (scampi)
4 tablespoons mayonnaise
2 tablespoons chili sauce
⅛ teaspoon Worcestershire sauce
⅛ teaspoon lemon juice

Cook scrubbed artichoke in 3″ boiling water until done (30-35 minutes); remove the tough outer leaves. Pull off remaining leaves and place inside up on a platter in attractive pattern like concentric circles. Drain shrimp and set aside. Mix together mayonnaise, chili sauce, Worcestershire sauce, and lemon juice. Put ⅛ teaspoon (a dab) on the meaty end of each leaf and top with a shrimp.

Make Ahead: Prepare party platter early in the day, cover with plastic wrap, and refrigerate. Artichoke can be cooked and refrigerated in cooking water for 2 days; sauce can also be prepared ahead.

Broccoli Canapés

Prep. 15 min. Makes 24 canapés.

Interesting blend of color and texture. Ideal for summer entertaining.

6 slices white bread, trimmed of crusts
2 heads fresh broccoli (1½-2 pounds)
2 tablespoons mayonnaise
1 tablespoon sour cream
½ teaspoon salt
1 teaspoon lemon juice
5 pieces pimiento, cut up (optional)

Cut bread into rounds with a 1″ cookie cutter. Use only dark green flowerets (not stem) of the broccoli; put into a bowl. Coat with mayonnaise, sour cream, salt, and lemon juice. Taste for seasoning. Spread on bread rounds, decorate each with pimiento piece, and serve.

Cherry Tomato Canapés

Prep. 30 min. Chill 2 hr. Makes 24.

A cool, colorful accompaniment to other hors d'oeuvres. Helps make an appetizing, festive platter.

2 dozen cherry tomatoes
6 ounces crab meat mixed with 2 tablespoons mayonnaise and 1 tablespoon chili sauce
> **OR**
3 tablespoons cream cheese mixed with 3 tablespoons Cheese with Fines Herbes (p. 78)

Hollow out cherry tomatoes leaving shells intact. A grapefruit sectioner and demitasse spoon can be useful. Place shells upside-down and chill for 30 minutes to an hour. Stuff with either crab, mayonnaise, chili sauce mixture or cheese combination. Chill until ready to serve.

Guacamole

Prep. 10 min. Makes 1 cup.

A hint of curry and green pepper zips up this favorite avocado dip.

1 large, ripe avocado
1 teaspoon finely minced onion
½ teaspoon curry powder
⅛ teaspoon garlic powder
2 tablespoons finely chopped green
    pepper
2 teaspoons lemon juice
3 tablespoons mayonnaise
Corn chips

Skin avocado and remove pit. Mash pulp with onion, curry, garlic, green pepper, and lemon juice. Just before serving stir in mayonnaise. Serve dip with chips.

Make Ahead: Dip keeps fresh for a day refrigerated in a covered container.

Pâté with Currants and Cognac
Prep. 20 min. Chill 2 hr. Makes about 1 cup.

Surprisingly easy to make in either a blender or food processor, but has a sophisticated taste. Make a double batch and use some in Filet of Beef en Papillote (p. 85).

½ cup currants
2 tablespoons cognac
1 pound chicken livers, fat removed
2 medium onions, finely chopped
½ cup butter
2 tablespoons cognac
1 teaspoon curry
Dash of salt and black pepper
¼ cup clarified butter

Soak currants in 2 tablespoons cognac for 15 minutes or more. Sauté livers and onions in ½ cup butter over low heat for about 10 minutes. Livers should be brown and well-cooked. Purée livers, onions, their juices, 2 tablespoons cognac, and curry in a blender or food processor (use steel knife) until smooth. Add salt and pepper to taste. Stir in currants and their marinating liquid. Put in a container and refrigerate 2 hours or until firm. Cover with ¼ cup clarified butter and chill.

Make Ahead: Refrigerate for up to 2 weeks or freeze in airtight container.

Note: Clarified butter is butter that has been melted and milk solids removed.

Pâté in Aspic
Prep. 15 min. Chill 3 hrs. Makes 3 cups.

A decorative, distinctive mold. The sherried aspic shows off the hearty pâté.

1 envelope unflavored gelatin
2 tablespoons water
2 cans (10¾ ounces each) condensed
    beef consommé
3 tablespoons sherry
6 ounces cream cheese
1½ pounds liverwurst
1 tablespoon brandy
3 tablespoons sherry

Soak gelatin in 2 tablespoons water. Heat undiluted consommé to a boil, add softened gelatin, stir thoroughly until dissolved, and add 3 tablespoons sherry. Pour ½ of gelatin liquid into the bottom of two or three 1½-cup glass dishes. Refrigerate until firm, at least half an hour. Keep rest of gelatin mixture at room temperature.

Use a food processor or egg beater to blend cream cheese and liverwurst into a smooth paste. Add brandy and 3 tablespoons sherry. Press liverwurst mixture on top of firm gelatin. Pour remaining consommé on top. Chill until firm, 2-3 hours. Loosen edges with a knife and invert onto a plate; serve with crackers.

Make Ahead: Stays fresh for 2 days in refrigerator. May be frozen in covered glass dishes for up to a month. Thaw at room temperature before unmolding.

Tiny Mushroom Tarts

Prep. 45 min. Cook 5 min. Makes 30 tarts.

This elegant presentation has a professional touch. Proves the home cook can cater with distinction.

Pastry for 9" pie crust (commercial or
  recipe p. 46)
½ pound fresh mushrooms
2 teaspoons minced onion
1 tablespoon butter
4 tablespoons Madeira
Salt and pepper
2 tablespoons light cream
2 teaspoons parsley

Roll dough out to ⅛" thickness on floured board. Cut with 3" cookie cutter (fluted if possible). Fit dough into greased 1¾" tartlet wells. Press down so there is no air between dough and pan. Grease outside bottom and sides of another tartlet pan and place over dough to keep it from rising. Bake at 400° for 8 minutes. Remove from oven, take off top pan, and prick dough several times with fork. Bake for an additional 4-6 minutes until golden. Cool slightly and loosen with knife. Cool on rack.

Wash, trim, and chop mushrooms finely with knife, or mince in blender or food processor. Cook onion in butter until transparent, about a minute. Add mushrooms and Madeira and cook until mushrooms are lightly browned, about 4 minutes. Add a pinch of salt and pepper. Add cream and cook over medium-low heat for another minute. Stir in parsley. Blend mixture until smooth. Fill pastry shells with mushroom paste.

Make Ahead: Unfilled shells can be frozen until firm and then transferred to airtight wrap and stacked in freezer. Defrost before filling.

Crisp Cheese Crackers

Prep. 40 min. Cook 15 min. Makes 50 crackers.

This gourmet cracker is fine to make ahead and keep for parties or unexpected guests.

2 sticks softened butter or margarine
2¼ cups grated sharp cheddar cheese
  (10 ounces)
½ teaspoon dry mustard
½ teaspoon onion salt
½ teaspoon Worcestershire sauce
4 drops Tabasco sauce
2 cups flour
2 cups crushed crisp rice cereal
50 pecan halves (optional)

Beat butter, cheese, mustard, onion salt, Worcestershire sauce, and Tabasco together. Add flour. Stir in crushed cereal. Chill for 20 minutes.

Preheat oven to 350°. Put round teaspoonfuls of dough onto lightly greased or nonstick cookie sheets. Use fork to flatten into cookie shapes. Decorate with pecan halves if desired. Bake for 15 minutes.

Make Ahead: Flavor improves if stored at room temperature for a day. Keeps well in an airtight container for a month or freezes for 2 months.

Cheese with Fines Herbes
Prep. 5 min. Makes 3 cups.

Delicious blend of cheeses and spices. Try as a dip for Beef Fondue or as stuffing for cherry tomatoes or mushrooms.

1 medium clove garlic
8 ounces unsalted butter
16 ounces cream cheese
¼ teaspoon thyme
¼ teaspoon basil
¼ teaspoon dill
¼ teaspoon oregano or marjoram

In a food processor (use steel knife) or blender mince garlic clove. Add remaining ingredients and blend until smooth. Serve with crackers or raw vegetables.

Make Ahead: Flavor improves if refrigerated for a day before serving. May be stored, covered, in refrigerator for 2 weeks.

Note: For a festive presentation, mound herbed cheese into a pineapple or bell shape. Rub 8 ounces smoked almonds between your hands to eliminate their salt and place flat side down to cover the cheese. Decorate the top with greenery. Chill. Take out of refrigerator a few hours before serving.

Cheese Pinwheels
Prep. 30 min. Chill 30 min. Cook 10

min. Makes 40-48 pinwheels.

Bacon, mustard, and cheeses make a savory appetizer in a pretty shape.

8 slices firm fresh white bread
2 tablespoons grated Parmesan cheese
1 cup grated sharp cheddar cheese
1 teaspoon Dijon mustard
1 teaspoon minced onion
5 tablespoons mayonnaise
2 tablespoons cooked, crumbled
   bacon (about 5 slices)

Trim crusts from bread and flatten bread with a rolling pin to ⅛" thickness. In a bowl, mix together cheeses, mustard, onion, and mayonnaise. Stir in bacon. Spread a heaping tablespoon of cheese mixture over entire surface of one slice of rolled-out bread. Start with a long side and roll bread up tightly. Keep the cheese inside and the plain bread outside, like a jelly roll. Refrigerate for 30 minutes or more. Slice each roll into 5 or 6 pieces. Lay each piece flat on a greased or nonstick cookie sheet and bake in preheated 350° oven for 10-12 minutes.

Make Ahead: Uncut pinwheel rolls and cut but unbaked pinwheels can be frozen in airtight wrap. Defrost and bake at 350° for 10-12 minutes.

Artichoke Balls
Prep. 15 min. Cook 10 min. Makes 2 dozen.

Tiny drop biscuits with a wonderful artichoke flavor set off by herbs and cheese.

1 can (8½ ounces) artichoke hearts, packed in water, drained
¼ cup butter or margarine, melted

1 tablespoon minced onion
⅛ teaspoon garlic powder
¼ teaspoon thyme
1 tablespoon grated cheddar cheese
½ cup crushed herb stuffing mix
1 egg, well beaten

Preheat oven to 350°. Finely chop artichoke hearts and cook briefly in butter with onion and garlic. Remove to a bowl. Add thyme, cheese, stuffing mix, and beaten egg. Put heaping teaspoonfuls of dough onto greased baking sheet. Bake for 10 minutes.

Make Ahead: Freezes well in airtight wrap.

Betsy's Shrimp Cocktail

Prep. 10 min. Makes about 70 hors d'oeuvres.

A dear friend, who also was the most organized person we knew, served this at her best parties.

2 pounds fresh, cooked, cleaned
   shrimp (large or medium size, about
   35 shrimp per pound), well chilled
½ cup chili sauce
¼ cup catsup
2 tablespoons lemon juice
1 teaspoon Worcestershire sauce
1 tablespoon horseradish
¼ teaspoon salt

Arrange shrimp on platter. Mix remaining ingredients together and put sauce in a bowl in the middle of platter. Spear shrimp with toothpicks and dip in sauce.

Make Ahead: Shrimp is highly perishable and loses flavor in freezing. Cooked shrimp can be stored covered in refrigerator, but for no more than 2 days.

Dinner

Soups

Minted Pea Soup

Prep. 10 min. Cook 42 min. Serves 8-10.

The artichoke cooking water gives this soup its distinctive flavor.

2 fresh artichokes, scrubbed clean
3 cups water
3 chicken bouillon cubes
½ medium onion, minced
2 tablespoons butter
1 package (10 ounces) frozen peas
1 teaspoon dried mint
½ cup heavy cream
Salt to taste
Pinch of freshly ground black pepper

Simmer artichokes, water, bouillon, and onion for 35 minutes. Add butter, peas, and mint and cook for 7 more minutes. Remove artichokes and 4 teaspoonfuls of peas and reserve. Purée remaining pea mixture in blender or food processor (use steel blade) until smooth. Strain purée through a sieve. Just before serving, add cream and salt and pepper. Garnish each serving with some of the reserved peas. Serve hot or cold.

Note: Cooked artichokes can be stored in the refrigerator and served at another meal or used in Party Artichokes and Shrimp (p. 75). If you have boiled artichokes in the previous 10 days, save 3 cups of the cooking water. Store covered in refrigerator. Fresh artichokes can then be omitted and boiling time reduced from 35 minutes to 10 minutes.

Watercress Soup

Prep. 15 min. Cook 27 min. Serves 10.

A nicely textured creamed vegetable soup.

¼ cup minced onion
1¾ cups peeled, chopped potatoes
2 tablespoons butter or margarine
3 cups peeled, chopped cucumbers
5 cups strong chicken stock or
  bouillon
2 cups watercress leaves (may include
  some tender stems)
1 cup light cream
Salt and pepper
Parsley or chives for garnish

Over low heat, sauté onion and potatoes in butter until onion is transparent, about 5 minutes. Add cucumbers and stock. Bring to a boil and simmer covered for 20 minutes. Add watercress. Simmer for 7 minutes more. Purée in blender or food processor until very smooth. Strain through a large sieve. Add cream and salt and pepper to taste. Either chill thoroughly or warm gently, as soup is good hot or cold. Sprinkle parsley or chives on top before serving.

Make Ahead: To store soup, refrigerate, or freeze purée *before* cream and garnish are added. Once frozen, defrost, stir in cream, and serve either warm or chilled.

Banana Bisque

Prep. 10 min. Chill 30 min. Serves 8.

An easy to make, refreshing beginning to a summer meal.

4 medium bananas
2 cups light cream
3 slices firm white bread
4 tablespoons butter or margarine
1 teaspoon cinnamon
1 tablespoon sugar

Mix peeled bananas and cream in blender or food processor until smooth. Cover and chill.

Trim crust from bread and cut bread into cubes. Melt butter and sauté bread until lightly browned on all sides. Mix cinnamon and sugar together and sprinkle over cubes. Place under broiler for a few seconds until sugar caramelizes. Just before serving, float croutons on soup.

Make Ahead: Soup can be prepared early in the day. Cooked croutons store well in airtight wrap in freezer.

Zucchini Soup

Prep. 10 min. Cook 10 min. Serves 6-8.

Our favorite, hot or cold.

3½ cups unpeeled, sliced zucchini
½ cup minced onions
2 cups chicken broth
1 teaspoon salt
⅛ teaspoon pepper
2 tablespoons butter
1½ cups light cream
6 to 8 teaspoons whipped or sour
  cream
2 teaspoons dill

Simmer zucchini, onions, broth, salt, and pepper until zucchini is tender, about 10 minutes. Cool slightly. Add butter. Purée mixture in blender or food processor (use steel blade). Just before serving, add light cream. Garnish each portion with a dollop of whipped or sour cream and a sprinkling of dill. (Whipped cream floats on soup better than sour cream.)

Make Ahead: Puréed zucchini mixture (before addition of cream) can be covered and refrigerated for 4 days or frozen in airtight container for a month.

Elegant Mushroom Consommé

Prep. 15 min. Cook 10 min. Serves 10.

A delicious, appealing light broth. Makes a pleasant prelude to a rich main course.

6 tablespoons butter
3 cups sliced fresh mushrooms
1 tablespoon minced onion
1 tablespoon flour
6 cups beef broth, stock, or bouillon
¼ cup sherry (cream or dry)
1 lemon, cut into 10 thin slices

Melt butter in a 2-quart saucepan; sauté mushrooms and onion for 7 minutes over low heat. Add flour and cook for another minute over low heat, stirring constantly. Pour in broth and sherry, bring to a boil, and simmer for 10 minutes. Pour into 10 soup bowls and float a slice of lemon on top of each.

Apple Artichoke Soup

Prep. 10 min. Cook 10 min. Serves 6.

So good and so simple.

2 tablespoons butter or margarine
2 tablespoons finely minced onion (or scallions)
¼ cup peeled, cored, and minced yellow apple

2 tablespoons flour
2 cups chicken broth
1 can (8½ ounces) artichoke hearts, packed in water, drained
1 tablespoon parsley
1 cup light cream
Salt and pepper

Melt butter over low heat and sauté onion and apple until soft, about 2 minutes. Add flour and cook over low heat for 2 minutes while stirring constantly. Add chicken broth, artichokes (reserve 2 for garnish), and parsley. Simmer for 10 minutes. Purée mixture in blender or food processor until smooth.

Just before serving add cream and salt and pepper to taste. Warm soup, but do not let it boil. Coarsely chop reserved artichokes and float on soup.

Make Ahead: May be made 2 days ahead and refrigerated, or frozen indefinitely in an airtight container *before* adding cream.

Fresh Tomato Soup

Prep. 30 min. Cook 1 hr. Serves 16.

This soup was created to use up extra garden tomatoes. Far superior in taste and nutrition to the canned variety.

4 tablespoons butter or margarine
½ cup coarsely diced celery
¼ cup minced onions
2 cups peeled, chopped potatoes (about 3 medium)
3 medium carrots, peeled and chopped
5 cups peeled, seeded, and coarsely cubed tomatoes (about 4 large)
6 cups chicken bouillon or stock
1 tablespoon brown sugar

1 bay leaf

½ teaspoon marjoram

½ teaspoon tarragon

Salt and pepper

1 cup heavy cream

Melt butter and sauté celery, onions, potatoes, and carrots for about 5 minutes, until lightly browned, while stirring frequently. Add tomatoes, stock, sugar, and herbs; simmer, covered, for 1 hour. Remove bay leaf and purée in blender or food processor until smooth. Strain. Add salt and pepper to taste. Add cream just before serving. Good either hot or cold.

Make Ahead: Puréed tomato mixture (before addition of cream) can be covered and refrigerated for 4 days or frozen in airtight container for three months.

Note: To peel tomatoes, plunge them in rapidly boiling water for 5 seconds. Remove with fork and put immediately in cold water. Peel off skin with a small knife.

Broccoli Soup

Prep. 10 min. Cook 20 min. Serves 10.

Broccoli, marjoram, and bacon are an ideal blend in this rich, smooth purée.

2 packages (10 ounces each) frozen broccoli, chopped or spears, or 1 large head fresh broccoli

3 cups water

3 chicken bouillon cubes

¼ cup minced onions

4 tablespoons butter or margarine

½ teaspoon salt

¾ cup minced, peeled potatoes

½ teaspoon marjoram

½ cup heavy cream

2 strips bacon, cooked crisp and crumbled

Simmer broccoli, water, bouillon, onions, butter, salt, potatoes, and marjoram, covered, until vegetables are tender, about 15-20 minutes. Purée broccoli mixture in blender or food processor until smooth. Just before serving add cream. Soup is good either hot or cold. Garnish each portion with sprinkling of bacon bits.

Make Ahead: Blended broccoli mixture (before addition of cream) can be covered and refrigerated for 4 days, or frozen in airtight container for three months.

Beef

Fail-Safe Roast Beef

Prep. 10 min. Cook 65 min. Serves 6-8.

A simple way to fix this popular roast. Wonderful with Herbed Popovers or Yorkshire Pudding (p. 57).

4-pound roast of beef (bottom rump, round, or sirloin tip), at room temperature

1 teaspoon salt

⅛ teaspoon pepper

Preheat oven to 475°. Rub salt and pepper all over roast. Place fat side up, in a deep pan (lined with foil for easy clean up). Cook for 20 minutes. Keep oven closed, lower heat to 350°, and cook 15 minutes for each pound after the first pound (i.e., 45 more minutes). Remove from oven and let stand for 15 minutes before carving. Meat will be rare.

Madeira Beef Gravy

2 cans (10½ ounces each) beef gravy
½ cup Madeira
Bouquet garni (1 bay leaf, ½ teaspoon dried parsley, ½ teaspoon
dried thyme tied in cheesecloth)

Combine gravy with Madeira. Add bouquet garni and simmer slowly for 30 minutes. Remove bag before serving gravy.

Regular Gravy

4 tablespoons pan drippings
4 tablespoons flour
2 cups beef stock or bouillon

In roasting pan mix drippings with flour. Cook and stir over low heat for 3 minutes. Slowly add beef stock and stir constantly until thickened. Strain and serve.

Oriental London Broil
Prep. 5 min. Marinate 2 hr. Cook 10 min. Serves 6-8.

Guaranteed to tenderize the toughest meat and add a special flavor. Try it with Rave Rice with Mushrooms (p. 103).

1 cup soy sauce
½ cup sugar
1 clove garlic, crushed
2 teaspoons freshly grated ginger
½ ounce bourbon
2-pound London broil steak

Mix first five ingredients together and pour over London broil in glass baking dish. Cover and refrigerate for 2 hours or longer, turning meat occasionally. Broil on second from top rack 5 minutes per side for rare. Brush with marinade while broiling. Cut meat on an angle into thin slices. Heat extra marinade and serve from a sauce boat if desired.

Make Ahead: Marinate beef for 2-4 hours. Drain, seal in airtight wrapping, and freeze.

Note: Fresh ginger root is available at many supermarkets. Store in an airtight bag in the freezer. Grate frozen ginger as needed; it will last indefinitely.

Variation: Another good beef marinade is made by mixing ½ cup soy sauce, ¼ cup gin, 1 tablespoon sugar, and 1 mashed garlic clove (or ⅛ teaspoon garlic powder). Use as described above.

Crockpot Beef Stroganoff
Prep. 15 min. Cook 8-10 hrs. Serves 10.

A fine company dish that can be adjusted to the cook's schedule.

3 pounds lean stewing beef, cut in 2″
pieces
2 tablespoons vegetable oil
1 cup chopped onions
1½ cups beef bouillon
½ cup dry vermouth
1 tablespoon Worcestershire sauce
¼ teaspoon garlic powder
1 pound fresh mushrooms, quartered
and sautéed
1 pound fresh carrots, peeled and cut
in pieces, or 2 small jars baby
carrots
2½ cups sour cream

¼ cup dry vermouth

Brown beef on all sides in hot oil. Remove meat and add onions to pan. Cook onions in oil over low heat until translucent, about 3 minutes.

Put meat, onions, bouillon, vermouth, Worcestershire sauce, and garlic powder in crockpot. Cook on low setting, covered, for 8-10 hours. During last hour of cooking add mushrooms and carrots; 15 minutes before serving, add sour cream and ¼ cup vermouth.

Make Ahead: Stroganoff may be cooked a day ahead, covered, and refrigerated. It may also be frozen in an airtight container *before* the addition of sour cream and vermouth. Defrost, add sour cream and vermouth, and warm at 300° for about 15 minutes, or until thoroughly heated.

Filet of Beef en Papillote
Prep. 15 min. Cook 10 min. Serves 4.

A fast way to serve individual Beef Wellingtons. Easy and elegant.

4 one-inch-thick filet mignon steaks, at room temperature
8 sheets filo dough
¾ cup pâté (p. 76), or 7-ounce can goose liver pâté
5 tablespoons melted butter
1 cup Blender Béarnaise (p. 85)

Preheat oven to 475°. Trim fat from steaks and place each on two sheets of filo dough. Cover top of meat generously with pâté. Enclose each steak in a drugstore wrap: bring up two sides of dough, fold together to form an airtight package, and tuck the ends

under the meat. Place on a well-buttered baking pan. Brush dough with melted butter. Bake for 10-12 minutes, depending on degree of rareness desired. Serve with Blender Béarnaise.

Beef Fondue
Prep. 15 min. Serves 4.

You deserve a break tonight; let your guests enjoy cooking together.

1 pound sirloin tips, cut into 1" squares
1 cup vegetable oil
½ cup Béarnaise sauce (p. 85)
½ cup cheese with fines herbes (p. 78), or commercial brand
½ cup barbecue sauce (p. 86), or commercial brand

Dry meat thoroughly. Heat oil in fondue pot. Cook meat on a fondue fork, one piece at a time, for as long as desired. Transfer to a cool fork and dip in one of the sauces.

Blender Béarnaise
Prep. 10 min. Makes ¾ cup.

This is so easy you will hope that no one asks for the recipe.

2 eggs yolks
1 tablespoon tarragon white wine vinegar
½ teaspoon salt
Dash of cayenne pepper
1 tablespoon tarragon
2 tablespoons chives
½ cup hot melted butter

Beat yolks, vinegar, salt, pepper, tarragon, and chives in a blender on high speed for 10 seconds. With blender still on add butter gradually in a continuous stream. Stop when all the butter is incorporated.

Make Ahead: Leftover sauce may be stored in refrigerator for 2 weeks.

Barbecue Sauce

Prep. 15 min. Age 2-4 weeks.

This spicy blend of flavors can be kept covered in the refrigerator for up to 3 months. Goes well with·pork, beef, or chicken.

1 bottle (28 ounces) catsup
1 bottle (12 ounces) chili sauce
⅓ cup prepared mustard
1 tablespoon dry mustard
1½ cups brown sugar
2 tablespoons coarsely ground pepper
1½ cups wine or cider vinegar
1 cup fresh lemon juice
½ cup steak sauce (A-1)
Dash of Tabasco sauce
¼ cup Worcestershire sauce
1 tablespoon soy sauce
1½ tablespoons vegetable oil
1 can (12 ounces) beer, light or dark

Mix all ingredients together. Cover and refrigerate for 2 weeks before using. Flavor improves with storage. A 4-week ripening period is ideal.

Veal Milanese

Prep. 10 min. Cook 10 min. Serves 6.

A gourmet treat that can be fixed at the last minute.

6 veal cutlets
¼ cup sweet sherry
½ cup seasoned bread or cracker crumbs
3 tablespoons olive oil

6 slices prosciutto
6 slices Swiss cheese

Cover cutlets with wax paper and pound until thin. Make small diagonal cuts in meat. Dip cutlets in sherry, then in crumbs, and sauté in hot oil over medium-high heat until veal is cooked, about 5 minutes. Remove from pan. Put a slice of prosciutto and cheese on each cutlet. Place briefly under broiler until cheese melts.

Note: For extra flavor, meat may be marinated in sherry for 1 hour before sautéeing.

Poultry and Pork

Fancy Herb Chicken Casserole

Prep. 10 min. Cook 1 hour. Serves 8.

A delectable, elegant company feast.

1 pound sliced mushrooms
½ cup chopped onions
6 tablespoons butter or margarine
1 package (6 ounces) wild or herb rice mix (raw, not instant or fast cooking)
1 teaspoon salt
¼ teaspoon pepper
3 cups cooked, cubed chicken (2 pounds cooked chicken breasts)
½ cup slivered almonds
1 cup medium cream
2 cups chicken broth
½ cup dry sherry
2 ounces shredded Swiss cheese

Preheat oven to 300°. Sauté mushrooms and onions in butter until tender, about 5 minutes. Mix with all other ingredients except cheese in a 3-quart casserole. Bake covered for 20 minutes. Uncover, sprinkle with cheese, and bake at 350° for 40-60 minutes.

Make Ahead: Bake casserole covered at 300° for 20 minutes. Cool and freeze in airtight container. Bake frozen uncovered for 1½ hours. Can also be prepared a day ahead, refrigerated, and warmed before serving.

Complete Chicken Casserole

Prep. 30 min. Cook 45 min. Serves 8-10.

An economical, tasty meal-in-a-pot, topped with a stuffing crust.

1 pound fresh mushrooms, trimmed
1 medium onion, finely chopped
2 tablespoons butter or margarine
1 tablespoon vegetable oil
6 cups chopped cooked chicken* or turkey meat
2 jars (16 ounces each) baby carrots, drained
2 cans (10¾ ounces each) cream of mushroom soup
¼ teaspoon sage
⅔ cup dry white wine
2 cups herb-seasoned stuffing mix (8 ounces)
⅓ cup butter or margarine (or amount in stuffing mix directions)

Sauté mushrooms and onion in butter and oil over medium heat until onion is limp and mushrooms are lightly browned. Arrange chicken, mushrooms, onion, and carrots in large, shallow casserole. Stir soup, sage, and wine together and pour over

chicken and vegetables.

Bake at 350° for 15 minutes. Make herb stuffing mix according to package directions. Spread stuffing evenly over chicken dish. Bake for 30 minutes more.

*Put two 3-pound frying chickens in soup kettle, add water to cover, bring to a boil, skim foam from top, reduce heat, and add 1 carrot, 1 onion, 1 bay leaf, and ¼ teaspoon thyme. Simmer covered for 30 minutes. Remove chicken from kettle, cool, discard skin and bones, and cut meat into bite-sized pieces.

Make Ahead: Cook casserole for 15 minutes. Then refrigerate or freeze *before* adding stuffing mixture. Casserole will keep for 2 days in refrigerator or a month in airtight container in freezer. Thaw, top with stuffing mixture, and cook for 30 minutes at 350°.

Note: To tenderize the meat, pour the wine-soup mixture over the cooked poultry a day ahead, cover, and refrigerate.

Chicken with Avocado and Almonds

Prep. 20 min. Cook 45 min. Serves 6-8.

A dish combining the best of a fricassee and chow mein. The avocados add striking color and flavor.

4 cups chicken broth
4 chicken bouillon cubes
½ cup slivered almonds
1 can (8 ounces) water chestnuts
3 to 4 cups chopped cooked chicken*
3 cups zucchini, unpeeled, cut into bite-sized pieces

½ cup margarine
½ cup flour
½ cup grated Monterey Jack cheese
2 medium avocados

Preheat oven to 350°. Heat broth and dissolve bouillon cubes. Spread almonds in single layer on cookie sheet and bake until lightly browned, about 5 minutes, and set aside. Drain water chestnuts and slice coarsely. Put chicken, zucchini, and chestnuts in large buttered casserole.

Melt margarine, add flour, and cook for 1 minute over low heat while stirring constantly. Add chicken broth slowly and cook and stir until the roux is smooth and thickened, about 5 minutes. Add sauce to casserole. Cook covered for 30 minutes. Sprinkle grated cheese on top. Cook uncovered another 15 minutes.

Peel and pit avocados, slice thinly and arrange pieces decoratively on top of chicken casserole. Sprinkle almonds over surface.

*Put 3-pound chicken in soup kettle, add water to cover, and bring to a boil. Skim foam from top, reduce heat, add ½ fresh lemon, 1 bay leaf, 1 clove, and stalk of celery, and simmer 30 minutes. Remove chicken from kettle, cool, discard skin and bones, and cut meat into bite-sized pieces. Reserve stock.

Make Ahead: Refrigerate, or freeze without avocados in airtight wrap. Defrost, warm, and put on avocados just before serving.

Note: To ripen hard avocado evenly put fruit in bag or dark place for a day or two.

Coq au Vin
Prep. 20 min. Cook 35 min. Serves 4.

A creamy wine sauce enhances the flavor of this savory chicken casserole.

3-pound frying chicken, quartered
2 tablespoons margarine
2 cups sliced mushrooms
10 to 16 small boiled onions (16-ounce jar)
¼ pound salt pork, rind removed, cut in half-inch pieces
1 tablespoon flour
⅛ teaspoon garlic powder
¼ teaspoon thyme
1½ cups red burgundy wine
4 tablespoons light cream

Preheat oven to 375°. Brown chicken on all sides in 1 tablespoon margarine, about 10 minutes, over medium heat. Meanwhile, in frying pan melt remaining 1 tablespoon margarine over medium heat and sauté mushrooms, boiled onions, and salt pork until lightly browned, about 5 minutes. Add flour, garlic powder, and thyme to mushroom mixture and cook for one more minute while stirring constantly.

Put chicken in casserole dish. Spread mushroom mixture around chicken. Pour in wine. Cook, covered, for 30 minutes, or until chicken is tender and its juices are clear yellow when chicken is pricked with a fork. Add cream and heat until warm.

Make Ahead: Freeze or refrigerate before adding cream. Cooked Coq au Vin can be refrigerated for 2 days or frozen in airtight containers for a month.

Note: Chicken may be cooked in a covered electric frying pan set at 375° instead of in the oven.

Family Favorite Fowl

Prep. 10 min. Cook 35 min. Serves 4.

Fast to prepare, light in calories, and still a crowd pleaser.

3-pound frying chicken, cut into
    serving pieces
1½ cups coarsely sliced fresh
    mushrooms
2 tablespoons margarine
1 tablespoon oil
Salt and pepper
1 tablespoon lemon juice
½ teaspoon dried tarragon
1 cup halved cherry tomatoes
⅓ cup dry white wine

Brown chicken quickly on all sides under broiler. Sauté mushrooms in 1 tablespoon margarine and oil until browned, about 5 minutes. Set aside.

Season chicken with salt and pepper to taste and arrange in a shallow casserole. Melt remaining tablespoon margarine. Mix with lemon juice and pour over chicken. Sprinkle with tarragon. Arrange tomatoes and mushrooms over and around chicken. Add wine.

Bake at 350°, basting occasionally, about 35-40 minutes until chicken is cooked and juices are clear yellow when chicken is pricked with a fork.

Chicken Cordon Rouge

Prep. 30 min. Cook 35 min. Serves 6.

Succulent individual servings that are as attractive to look at as they are delicious to eat.

3 whole chicken breasts, skinned, boned,
    and halved
Salt and freshly ground black pepper
6 tablespoons butter or margarine,
    softened
6 small slices lean ham (cooked)
6 small slices mozzarella, fontina, or pro-
    volone cheese
1 tablespoon dried parsley
1 teaspoon dried marjoram
¼ teaspoon dried thyme
½ cup flour
2 eggs, well beaten
1 cup fresh bread crumbs
½ cup dry white wine or vermouth

Preheat oven to 350°. Put each breast between pieces of wax paper and pound to ⅛″ thickness. Season with salt and pepper. Spread 2 tablespoons softened butter on the meat. Place sliced ham and cheese in the center of each breast. Roll up each breast jelly-roll fashion and tuck in the ends. Mix herbs with flour. Dredge chicken in seasoned flour, dip in beaten eggs, then cover with bread crumbs. Place rolls, seam side down, in baking dish. Melt remaining 4 tablespoons butter and pour over chicken. Bake for 15 minutes. Pour wine over chicken and bake for 20 minutes more.

Make Ahead: Cook chicken rolls without wine at 350° for 20 minutes only. Cool, cover pan with airtight wrap, and freeze. To serve, defrost, pour wine over chicken, and cook at 350° for 15 minutes.

Microwave: Pour wine over frozen rolls and cook on high for 4 minutes. Turn the pan 180° and cook for 4 minutes longer.

Quick Picnic Chicken

Prep. 10 min. Cook 1 hr. Serves 4.

A cinch to prepare. Subtly flavored fried chicken without the fuss of oil frying.

3-pound frying chicken, cut in serving pieces, or 2 whole breasts
Salt and pepper
1½ tablespoons mayonnaise
1½ tablespoons sour cream
½ teaspoon curry powder
1 cup herb stuffing mix, dry

Preheat oven 350°. Season chicken with salt and pepper. Mix mayonnaise, sour cream, and curry together and spread over chicken. Crush dry stuffing mix in blender or food processor and coat chicken with stuffing crumbs.

Bake chicken, skin side up, for about 1 hour, or until chicken is tender and juices are clear yellow when meat is pricked with a fork. Do not turn chicken during cooking. Good either hot or cold.

Make Ahead: Chicken may be cooked and refrigerated a day before it is used.

Chicken with Wine and Tomatoes

Prep. 25 min. Cook 45 min. Serves 4-6.

This dish tastes much better if made a day ahead and reheated before serving.

3-pound frying chicken, cut in serving pieces, or 3 breasts, halved
½ cup flour
1½ teaspoons dried basil
1 teaspoon salt
½ teaspoon freshly ground black pepper
¼ cup olive oil
½ cup margarine
¾ cup dry vermouth
2 cups canned Italian pear tomatoes, undrained, cut into cubes
2 tablespoons margarine
1 tablespoon oil
½ pound fresh mushrooms, sliced
2 tablespoons minced onion
¼ teaspoon powdered garlic, or 2 cloves fresh garlic, finely chopped

Shake each chicken piece in a bag that contains a mixture of flour, basil, salt, and pepper. Reserve leftover flour mixture. Heat olive oil and ½ cup margarine in frying pan and brown the floured chicken on all sides. Transfer chicken to covered casserole and stir leftover seasoned flour into fat left in frying pan. Gradually stir in vermouth. Cook over low heat until the sauce is thickened and smooth, about 5 minutes. Mix sauce and tomatoes together and pour over chicken.

In separate pan, melt 2 tablespoons margarine and 1 tablespoon oil and sauté mushrooms until lightly browned, about 5 minutes. Remove mushrooms and sauté onion and garlic until onion is transparent, about 3 minutes. Spread mushrooms, onion, and garlic over chicken.

Bake at 350° for about 45 minutes, covered, until chicken is tender and juices are clear when chicken is pricked with a fork.

Make Ahead: Flavor is significantly improved with early cooking. To freeze, wrap securely in airtight wrap after cooking. Defrost and warm at 350° for 15 minutes.

Easy Pork in Wine

Prep. 10 min. Cook 45 min. Serves 2.

Combine ordinary ingredients simply to prepare an exotic dish.

2 lean pork chops
Salt and pepper to taste
1 tablespoon cooking oil (optional)
2 tablespoons chili sauce
¼ cup dry vermouth

Preheat oven to 350°. Trim fat from pork chops. Season meat with salt and pepper. Either brown chops in hot oil or broil briefly on both sides to save calories. Put chops in baking dish and cover them with chili sauce and wine. Bake covered for 45 minutes.

Barbecued Pork Ribs

Prep. 20 min. Marinate overnight. Cook 8 min. Serves 4-6.

Best if made a day ahead so sauce can permeate the meat.

3 to 4 pounds country-style pork ribs
   or spareribs
1 teaspoon vinegar
1 medium onion, finely minced
½ cup light or dark brown sugar
1 tablespoon barbecue spice
1 tablespoon prepared yellow
   mustard
2 tablespoons Worcestershire sauce
1 bottle (14 ounces) catsup

Cut excess fat from meat. Boil ribs in enough water to cover, flavored with vinegar, for 20 minutes. Mix together onion, sugar, spice, mustard,

Worcestershire sauce, and catsup. Marinate meat in sauce overnight. Broil ribs or cook over charcoal fire for about 4 minutes per side. Occasionally brush ribs with extra sauce.

Make Ahead: Boil ribs and cover with sauce. Meat will keep in freezer in airtight container for up to two weeks. To serve, thaw and broil or cook over charcoal until heated through.

Pork and Peaches

Prep. 15 min. Cook 50 min. Serves 4-6.

Striking, tasty, and colorful.

6 good lean pork chops
Salt and pepper
2 cups orange juice
2 tablespoons vinegar
2 teaspoons cinnamon
1 can (29 ounces) yellow cling peach
   halves

Trim fat from pork, season with salt and pepper, and brown quickly under the broiler. Combine juice, vinegar, and cinnamon.

Preheat oven to 325°. Put chops in ovenproof casserole, place a peach on each, and pour juice mixture over all. Bake uncovered for 50 minutes until meat is fork tender.

Make Ahead: Refrigerate cooked meat in sauce for a day or freeze cooked meat and sauce in airtight container. Thaw and heat in a 300° oven for 15 minutes. Peaches don't freeze well.

Pork Tenderloin with Cointreau

Prep. 15 min. Cook 45 min. Serves 4.

The choice of fresh fruit gives variety, color, and texture to the sauce, which is a delicate blend of orange and pork.

1½ to 2 pounds pork tenderloin, cut in 1-inch pieces (3 cups meat)
½ cup flour
1 teaspoon salt
¼ teaspoon pepper
3 tablespoons butter or margarine
1½ cups condensed beef consommé (10¾-ounce can)
½ cup water
1 cup green seedless grapes, or 1 cup fresh, pitted red cherries
2 tablespoons soft butter or margarine
2 tablespoons flour
4 to 5 tablespoons Cointreau

Dredge pork pieces in flour mixed with salt and pepper. Sauté meat in 3 tablespoons butter until lightly browned on all sides, about 6 minutes. Drain off all excess fat in pan. Add consommé, water, and cherries (if using them) to meat. Simmer covered for 30 minutes. Mix thoroughly 2 tablespoons soft butter and 2 tablespoons flour, add to consommé, and stir well. Add grapes (if using them) and Cointreau, and simmer for an additional 15 minutes.

Sherried Pork Chops

Prep. 5 min. Cook 1 hr. Serves 4-6.

A favorite for all ages. Simple ingredients are transformed into a real treat.

4 to 6 good lean pork chops
Salt and pepper
¼ teaspoon dried basil
½ cup water
½ cup dry sherry
1 cup applesauce

Trim fat from chops. Season with salt and pepper, and brown both sides quickly under the broiler. Sprinkle chops with basil. Simmer chops in water and sherry in a covered pan for 45 minutes. Turn chops over, cover tops with applesauce, and continue simmering for about 15 minutes more until chops are fork tender and applesauce is warm.

Baked Ham with Maple and Port

Prep. 10 min. Cook 1 hr. Serves 12-14.

Maple and port combine in a flavorful, aromatic coating for a baked ham.

4-pound fully cooked top quality boneless ham
½ cup maple syrup
¼ cup port

Preheat oven to 325°. Score ham (make diagonal intersecting lines that form x's all over ham). Mix maple syrup and port together. Place ham on a rack in an uncovered roasting pan and pour maple/port mixture over it. Bake for about an hour (15 minutes per pound) until ham is heated through (meat thermometer reads 130°). Baste occasionally. For easier carving, let ham sit for 15 minutes.

Make Ahead: Baked ham will stay fresh in refrigerator for at least a week.

Note: Many butchers will cut ham in thin slices after you have cooked it.

"No. 3" or "No. 4" sized slices can be rolled, decorated with parsley, and served with party rye bread.

Ham and Green Bean Casserole

Prep. 15 min. Chill 6 hr. Cook 50 min. Serves 6.

A mock soufflé which won't collapse between oven and table. A complete meal-in-one dish.

1 package (10 ounces) frozen green beans
2 tablespoons butter or margarine
6 slices white bread, trimmed of crusts
2 cups cubed cooked ham
5 ounces cheddar cheese, grated
1½ cups milk
3 eggs, slightly beaten
1 teaspoon Dijon mustard
1 tablespoon dried minced onion
1 teaspoon onion salt
¼ cup port or cream sherry

Cook beans according to package directions. Drain well. Spread butter on bread and cut into cubes. Grease a shallow baking dish. Cover bottom with bread cubes, add the beans, and place the ham on top. Sprinkle with cheese. Mix milk, beaten eggs, mustard, onion, onion salt, and port or sherry together and pour over layered ingredients. Refrigerate for at least 6 hours or overnight. Bake uncovered at 325° for 50 minutes.

Fish and Seafood

Sherried Shad Roe

Prep. 5 min. Cook 20 min. Serves 2.

A nice combination of flavors that sets off the roe.

1 large pair or set of roe
¼ cup butter
3 tablespoons dry sherry
3 tablespoons Marsala
1 tablespoon lemon juice
4 bacon strips, cooked
2 slices toast

Sauté roe in melted butter for 8 minutes on each side. Transfer to heated serving dish. Add sherry, Marsala, and lemon juice to pan and boil down liquids rapidly until volume is halved. Pour sauce over roe. Serve on toast. Garnish with bacon strips.

Shrimp Tempura

Prep. 20 min. Cook 10 min. Serves 4.

A delightful version of this Japanese dish.

16 large fresh shrimp with tails
2 small zucchini
1 small eggplant
1 egg, beaten
1 cup flour
½ teaspoon salt
⅞ cup water
2 cups vegetable oil for frying
¼ cup soy sauce
1 tablespoon white wine
½ cup water
1 teaspoon sugar
½ teaspoon powdered ginger

Clean shrimp and butterfly them. (Leave tails on, cut along backs, and flatten.) Cut zucchini and eggplant into thin slices.

Mix egg, flour, salt, and ⅞ cup water lightly with fork. Dip shrimp and vegetables in batter to cover. Fry in 2″ oil heated to 400° in electric skillet until shrimp are golden brown on one side. Turn and cook the other side. Drain well.

Simmer soy sauce, wine, ½ cup water, sugar, and ginger together and stir until smooth. Use warm sauce as a dip.

Sensational Swordfish or Scrod

Prep. 5 min. Cook 10 min. Serves 2.

A perfectly blended herb coating for wine-braised fish.

¾-inch-thick piece of swordfish or scrod (about 1 pound)
¼ cup mayonnaise
¼ teaspoon thyme
¼ teaspoon basil
½ teaspoon parsley
¾ cup dry vermouth

Place fish in a buttered shallow ovenproof pan. Mix mayonnaise and herbs. Spread herb mixture over fish and pour vermouth around it, so that the liquid comes almost halfway up the side of the fish. Broil on second from top rack in oven 10-15 minutes. Fish will feel springy. No need to turn fish over.

Microwave: Cook in a covered dish for 5 minutes 30 seconds on high. Rotate ¼ turn after every 2 minutes. Broil on top rack of conventional oven for about 2½ minutes until top is brown.

Georgian Shrimp Casserole

Prep. 20 min. Cook 55 min. Serves 6-8.

Casserole improves in flavor if kept in refrigerator for a day before baking.

1 cup raw rice (not fast-cooking)
2½ cups water
¼ cup chopped onion
1 teaspoon salt
Dash of cayenne pepper
⅛ teaspoon mace
2 tablespoons butter
2 pounds large, shelled, cleaned, cooked shrimp
1 teaspoon lemon juice
½ cup sliced celery
3 tablespoons vegetable oil
1 can (10¾ ounces) tomato soup
1 cup heavy cream
½ cup dry vermouth
3 tablespoons chili sauce

Simmer rice, covered, in water for 20 minutes, and drain. In a casserole, sauté onion seasoned with salt, cayenne pepper, and mace in butter for 5 minutes. Add shrimp, lemon juice, celery, oil, and rice. Stir in undiluted soup, cream, vermouth, and chili sauce. Bake uncovered at 350° for 55 minutes.

Make Ahead: Before baking, casserole can be frozen and then baked frozen at 350° for 1½-1¾ hours.

Saffron Shrimp

Prep. 15 min. Cook 1 hr. Serves 6.

A colorful dish for a buffet.

2 cups large, shelled, deveined shrimp
2 cups cooked saffron-flavored rice
¼ pound butter, melted
1 cup heavy cream
½ teaspoon Worcestershire sauce
½ cup chili sauce
¼ teaspoon Tabasco
Salt and pepper

Put shrimp (cooked according to package directions or boiled in water for 2 minutes if fresh), cooked rice, and all other ingredients in a large covered casserole, and mix well. Bake at 325° for 1 hour, covered.

Louisiana Shrimp
Prep. 20 min. Cook 30 min. Serves 6.

A spicy Creole sauce complements the shrimp and vegetables.

2 pounds large shrimp
½ cup minced onion
1 pound mushrooms, sliced
4 tablespoons butter or margarine
2 tablespoons oil
1 can (10¾ ounces) tomato soup
1 can (5 ounces) beef consommé
1 teaspoon Worcestershire sauce
1 teaspoon curry powder
1 tablespoon sugar

Simmer shrimp in water to cover for 5 minutes. Drain, shell, and devein. Set aside.

In a *large* frying pan sauté onion and mushrooms in butter and oil over low heat until onion is transparent, about 5 minutes. Drain mushrooms and onion and add undiluted soups. Stir in Worcestershire sauce,

curry powder, and sugar. Simmer for 20 minutes. Add shrimp and simmer for 10 more minutes. Serve over rice.

Crab Casserole
Prep. 30 min. Bake 40 min. Serves 12.

When cooked in the rich, creamy sauce, langostino tastes as good as crab and is a lot cheaper.

12 ounces sliced mushrooms
2 tablespoons butter or margarine, melted
1 tablespoon oil
1 can (8 ounces) water chestnuts, drained and sliced
6 tablespoons butter or margarine
⅓ cup "instantized" flour (like Wondra)
1 can (10¾ ounces) chicken broth
1 cup light cream
½ cup dry sherry
½ teaspoon nutmeg
1½ pounds crab meat or langostino
1 tablespoon butter, melted
½ cup bread crumbs
2 tablespoons grated Swiss cheese

Sauté mushrooms in 2 tablespoons melted butter and the oil until browned, about 5 minutes. Mix with sliced water chestnuts. Set aside.

Melt 6 tablespoons butter, add flour, and cook over low heat for 2 minutes while stirring constantly. Add chicken broth, cream, sherry, and nutmeg. Cook over low heat while stirring constantly until thickened and smooth. Mix sauce with crab meat or langostino and remove from heat. Stir in mushrooms and water chestnuts.

Put crab mixture in shallow casserole. Mix 1 tablespoon melted butter, crumbs, and cheese and sprinkle over crab. Bake uncovered at 350° for 40 minutes.

Make Ahead: Prepare casserole but do not bake. Instead, freeze in airtight container. Cook frozen casserole at 325° for 60-70 minutes.

Swiss Scallops
Prep. 10 min. Cook 5 min. Serves 4.

Perfect for the tired and hungry. It almost makes itself.

1½ pounds sea scallops
Salt and pepper
½ cup dry vermouth
3 tablespoons grated Swiss cheese
3 tablespoons chopped parsley

Wash, dry, and cut scallops into bite-sized pieces. Season with salt and pepper. Spread scallops in a single layer and spoon ¼ cup vermouth over them. Broil for 2 minutes on the top oven rack. Turn scallops over, cover with remaining vermouth, and sprinkle with cheese. Broil for 3 or 4 minutes more, until scallops are tender. Garnish with parsley.

Vegetables

Hasty Corn Pudding
Prep. 5 min. Cook 45 min. Serves 6.

Be sure pudding is cooked in a dish where it will be 1½ inches deep. Otherwise baking times change.

2 cans (17 ounces each) creamed corn
3 eggs

1 tablespoon melted butter or margarine
⅔ cup milk
¼ cup sugar
1 teaspoon salt
½ teaspoon paprika

Preheat oven to 375°. Beat all ingredients except paprika together until well blended. Pour corn mixture into shallow, buttered baking dish. Sprinkle paprika on top. Bake uncovered until firm, about 45-60 minutes.

Microwave: Cook on high for 25 minutes. Rotate ¼ turn every 5 minutes. Leave in oven an additional 2-3 minutes after cooking.

Crunchy Green Beans
Prep. 15 min. Cook 30 min. Serves 6-8.

A fine way to dress up a plain meal.

4 packages (10 ounces each) frozen French-cut green beans, cooked, or 3 cans (16 ounces each)
1 medium onion, minced
1 tablespoon butter or margarine, melted
1½ cups sour cream
1 cup grated Swiss cheese (4 ounces)
⅛ teaspoon dried dill
3 tablespoons butter or margarine
¾ cup coarsely crumbled potato chips

Drain beans and set aside. Sauté onion in 1 tablespoon melted butter until onion is soft and transparent, about 3 minutes. Mix onion, beans, sour cream, cheese, and dill and put in greased shallow 2-quart casserole. Dot with 3 tablespoons butter and sprinkle with potato chips. Bake uncovered at 325° for 30 minutes.

Peas Alaska

Prep. 15 min. Cook 5 min. Serves 6.

The velvet texture and color contrast between peas and topping make this an unusual vegetable dish. It is also good without the topping.

1 large package (20 ounces) frozen
  peas
½ teaspoon salt
1 teaspoon sugar
¼ teaspoon marjoram
2 tablespoons butter
¼ cup light cream
¼ cup sour cream
Salt and pepper
1 egg white
1 tablespoon sugar

Cook peas according to package directions, but season cooking water with salt, sugar, and marjoram. Drain peas when tender. Purée peas, butter, cream, and sour cream in blender or food processor until smooth. Season to taste with salt and pepper. Warm and serve as is, or beat egg white until soft peaks form. Add sugar and beat until stiff peaks form. Spread on top of warm purée. Broil 3 inches from heating element for 2-3 minutes until meringue is light brown. Serve immediately.

Make Ahead: Pea purée can be made early in the day and refrigerated until shortly before serving.

Citrus Carrots

Prep. 10 min. Cook 35 min. Serves 6.

A hint of tangy lemon distinguishes this dish.

2 pounds fresh carrots
¼ cup butter or margarine
2 tablespoons sugar
1 cup water
1 lemon rind
½ teaspoon salt
Dash of pepper
2 tablespoons butter
1 tablespoon parsley
2 teaspoons lemon juice (optional)

Peel and slice carrots. Combine ¼ cup butter, sugar, water, rind of an entire lemon, salt, and pepper. Bring to a boil. Add carrots, cover pan, and simmer for 35-40 minutes, or until tender. Drain carrots and remove lemon rind. Toss carrots in 2 tablespoons butter, parsley, and lemon juice if desired.

Make Ahead: Carrots may be cooked several hours early and left at room temperature in cooking water. Reheat, drain, and toss in butter and parsley.

Microwave: Cook ½ recipe at a time. Cook on high for 8 minutes.

Chinese Celery

Prep. 10 min. Cook 30 min. Serves 6.

Refreshingly different. Subtle flavor with lots of crunch.

2 cups celery cut in 1″ pieces (about 8
  stalks)
1 cup chicken broth
1 can (8 ounces) water chestnuts,
  drained and sliced

½ cup blanched slivered almonds

2 tablespoons cornstarch, softened in
   3 tablespoons cold white wine

¼ teaspoon rosemary

2 tablespoons butter or margarine,
   melted

½ cup seasoned bread crumbs

Simmer celery in broth until celery is tender but still crisp, about 5 minutes. Remove celery and cool broth. Mix celery, chestnuts, and almonds, and place in shallow greased casserole.

Dissolve softened cornstarch and wine in cold broth, add rosemary, and boil, stirring constantly, until thickened, about 1 minute. Pour broth over vegetables, mix butter with bread crumbs, and sprinkle over celery. Bake uncovered at 350° for 30 minutes.

Cheddar Eggplant

Prep. 20 min. Cook 30 min. Serves 6.

A light, soufflé-like way to serve eggplant.

2 small eggplants, peeled and cut
   into slices ¼″ thick

2 tablespoons vegetable oil

Salt and pepper

8 slices firm white toast

2 tablespoons butter

2 cups grated cheddar cheese

1 egg

1 cup milk

¼ teaspoon marjoram

Spread eggplant slices on cookie sheet, brush them with oil, and season with salt and pepper. Broil on top rack of oven until tops are lightly browned, about 4 minutes. Turn egg-

plants over, brush with oil, season, and broil again until tops are light brown, about 3 minutes.

Trim crusts from toast. Butter and cut each slice into eighths. Into a well-greased casserole layer half the toast, eggplant, and cheese. Repeat layers with remaining toast, eggplant, and cheese.

Beat egg with a fork or whisk until light. Mix in milk and marjoram. Pour egg mixture over casserole. Bake at 375° for 30 minutes.

Make Ahead: Ingredients can be layered in casserole and refrigerated for a day, but do not add beaten egg, milk, and marjoram until just before cooking.

Baked Tomatoes Fondue

Prep. 10 min. Cook 1 hr. Serves 10.

An easy variation of stewed tomatoes, but with a special blend of seasonings.

2½ cups whole tomatoes in purée
   (28-ounce can)

2 slices firm white bread, trimmed of
   crusts

½ cup chopped celery

1 tablespoon minced onion

1 teaspoon salt

⅛ teaspoon freshly ground pepper

2 tablespoons sugar

½ teaspoon basil

2 tablespoons parsley

1 tablespoon butter or margarine

Cut tomatoes in large pieces and reserve with purée. Crumble bread. Stir tomatoes and purée, bread, celery, onion, salt, pepper, sugar, and herbs together and put into a greased 2-quart casserole. Dot with butter. Bake at 325° for 1 hour uncovered. Stir occasionally.

Make Ahead: Cook and refrigerate the day before serving if desired.

Cheese Tomatoes

Prep. 10 min. Cook 30 min. Serves 4-6.

A hearty, filling vegetable preparation. No need for potatoes with this dish.

2 tablespoons minced onion
1 tablespoon butter or margarine
3 cups undrained, canned tomatoes
 (28 ounces)
¾ cup herbed stuffing mix
⅛ teaspoon garlic powder
¼ teaspoon thyme
½ cup grated cheddar cheese
1 tablespoon butter

Sauté onion in 1 tablespoon melted butter until soft, about 3 minutes. Stir in tomatoes with juice, stuffing, garlic powder, and thyme. Spoon into shallow greased casserole. Sprinkle grated cheese on top and dot with 1 tablespoon butter. Bake at 350° for half an hour.

Artichoke Hearts and Mushrooms with Hollandaise

Prep. 10 min. Cook 5 min. Serves 4-6.

An unforgettable, instant creation that adds a regal touch to any meal.

3 cups artichoke hearts (two 14-
 ounce cans, packed in water)
1 pound fresh mushrooms, quartered
2 tablespoons butter or margarine

1 tablespoon oil
Hollandaise Sauce (see below)

Drain water from artichokes. Sauté mushrooms in 2 tablespoons butter and oil until lightly browned, about 5 minutes. Arrange mushrooms and artichokes in a single layer in a shallow casserole. Pour Hollandaise Sauce over vegetables and warm at 350° for about 5 minutes.

Hollandaise Sauce

4 egg yolks
½ cup butter or margarine
½ teaspoon fresh lemon juice

Put yolks in blender. Melt ½ cup butter over low heat until hot and bubbly but do not let it brown. Start blender and slowly pour in butter and lemon juice. Blend for 5 seconds more.

Note: Mushrooms brown better if not crowded in a pan, so use a couple of frying pans to sauté them simultaneously.

Zucchini Casserole

Prep. 20 min. Cook 30 min. Serves 6.

A smooth cream sauce highlighted by dill contrasts beautifully with the crisp zucchini and moist stuffing crust.

1½ pounds zucchini or yellow
 squash, unpeeled
1 tablespoon dried dill
¾ teaspoon garlic powder
Salt and pepper
3 tablespoons butter or margarine
2 tablespoons flour
⅔ cup milk
1 cup herbed stuffing mix
3 tablespoons butter or margarine

Trim off ends and cut zucchini into bite-sized pieces. Cover with water, stir in dill and garlic, and simmer for 3 minutes. Cover, reduce heat, and simmer until zucchini is tender, about 5 minutes. Reserve cooking water. Pat zucchini dry, season with salt and pepper to taste, and put in greased shallow casserole.

Melt 3 tablespoons butter over low heat, add flour, and cook for 2 minutes, stirring constantly. Add milk and continue cooking and stirring until sauce is blended and thickened — about 5 minutes. Lightly mix with zucchini.

Make stuffing mix according to package directions using butter and the water in which zucchini was cooked as liquid. Spread dressing over zucchini. Bake at 350° for 30 minutes.

Make Ahead: Zucchini and cream sauce can be made early in the day, covered, and refrigerated. It can also be frozen, defrosted, and baked at 350° for 30 minutes. Stuffing will be better if stored separately from zucchini and spread on casserole just before baking.

Suisse Zucchini
Prep. 15 min. Cook 30 min. Serves 4.

A simple, straightforward way of bringing out the best in zucchini.

2 pounds zucchini
1 teaspoon salt
3 tablespoons minced onion
3 tablespoons sour cream
3 tablespoons grated Gruyère or
    Swiss cheese
Salt and pepper

2 tablespoons milk
2 tablespoons melted butter

Wash zucchini and trim off ends. Boil slowly in 1 quart water and 1 teaspoon salt, for 8 minutes uncovered. Drain and slice into ½" thick pieces.

Preheat oven to 350°. Butter a 2-quart casserole. Cover the bottom with ⅓ of the zucchini slices. Sprinkle 1 tablespoon onion on top, dot with 1 tablespoon sour cream, and sprinkle with 1 tablespoon cheese. Season lightly with salt and pepper. Repeat for two more layers.

Pour milk and melted butter on top of last layer. Bake uncovered for 30 minutes.

Zucchini with Watercress
Prep. 15 min. Cook 5 min. Serves 4-6.

A silky, rich casserole with a crisp topping.

2 pounds zucchini, unpeeled
1 teaspoon salt
1 cup watercress leaves, including
    tender stems (1 bunch with 1½" diameter across width of stems)
4 tablespoons butter
⅓ cup heavy cream
3 tablespoons sugar
½ teaspoon salt
Dash of pepper
3 tablespoons fresh bread crumbs or
    slivered almonds

Wash zucchini and trim off ends. Boil slowly in 1 quart water and 1 teaspoon salt for 4 minutes. Add watercress and boil for 4 more minutes. Drain and coarsely chop. Add butter, cream, sugar, salt, and pepper to zucchini and watercress and purée in blender or food processor until smooth.

Put purée in greased casserole. Sprinkle bread crumbs or almonds on top. Heat at 350° for 5-10 minutes, or until warm.

Make Ahead: Purée can be made early in the day, covered, and refrigerated. Purée also freezes well in an airtight container. Defrost and warm or heat frozen in the top of a double boiler. Top with bread crumbs or almonds just before serving.

Note: If watercress is not available, simply boil zucchini for 8 minutes and proceed with recipe.

Spinach Pie

Prep. 45 min. Cook 45 min. Serves 14.

Excellent for a crowd. May be a main dish for lunch or a spectacular addition to dinner. A nutritious napoleon.

3 packages (10 ounces each) frozen
    chopped spinach
¾ cup chopped onions
½ cup butter or margarine
1 bunch chopped parsley (stems together are 1″ in diameter)
1½ teaspoons salt
½ teaspoon black pepper
1 teaspoon dill
1½ cups sour cream
3 eggs
1 pound filo dough
½ cup melted butter or margarine

Preheat oven to 350°. While partially defrosting the spinach, sauté onions in butter until limp; add parsley, salt, pepper, and dill. Cut spinach into cubes. Over high heat, stir-fry the spinach and onion mixture until spinach is fully thawed and all water has evaporated. Remove pan from heat, stir in sour cream, and cool. Beat eggs until frothy and mix with spinach. Use scissors to cut 20 sheets of filo dough to fit a 13″x9″ pan. Brush 10 sheets lightly with melted butter and layer in pan, buttered side up. Spread spinach mixture evenly on top. Lightly butter 10 more sheets of dough and put them over spinach, buttered side up; if desired, score through top layers of dough with a knife to make an attractive design. Bake for 45-50 minutes, or until dough is golden.

Make Ahead: Pie may be made early in the day, covered, and refrigerated until time to bake.

Baked Mushrooms Flambé

Prep. 15 min. Cook 15 min. Serves 4.

A rich and sumptuous medley of flavors.

8 large mushrooms
4 tablespoons butter
3 tablespoons finely chopped onion
1½ slices white bread
¼ teaspoon salt
¼ cup brandy
1 cup heavy cream

Preheat oven to 350°. Wash and dry mushrooms. Pull out stems and chop them finely. Melt butter in a small frying pan. Sauté onion and chopped mushroom stems until limp, about 4 minutes. Crumb bread in food processor or blender. Add crumbs and salt to onion mixture and cook for 2 minutes over medium-low heat. Pour warm brandy into pan, and using a long-handled match, set fire to the mushroom mixture. Carefully shake pan to distribute flame evenly.

Peel thin outer layer from mushroom caps. Place cavity side up in an ovenproof dish. Stuff caps with sautéed mushroom mixture. Gently pour cream over caps. Bake for 15-20 minutes. Baste once or twice.

Broccoli, Mushroom, Artichoke Supreme

Prep. 20 min. Cook 45 min. Serves 6-8.

A delectable vegetable flan to serve as either a luncheon meal or dinner side dish.

2½ cups quartered fresh mushrooms
¾ cup minced onion
1 tablespoon vegetable oil
2 tablespoons butter or margarine
1 package (10 ounces) frozen
    chopped broccoli
1 cup grated Swiss cheese
5 eggs, beaten until foamy
5 canned artichoke hearts, packed in
    water, drained

Preheat oven to 350°. Sauté mushrooms and onion in oil and melted butter until mushrooms are lightly browned, about 5 minutes. Stir occasionally. Remove from heat. Meanwhile cook broccoli according to package directions. Drain well. Mix broccoli and cheese with mushrooms and onions. Add well-beaten eggs and put in greased shallow casserole. Decorate top with large artichoke

pieces. Cover and bake for 40 minutes. Uncover and bake 5 more minutes, until top is lightly browned.

Make Ahead: All ingredients except eggs can be cooked, assembled, and refrigerated a day early. Beat eggs and mix in just before cooking. Leftovers can be frozen in airtight container. Bake frozen at 350° for about 15 minutes or thaw and bake for 10 minutes.

Stuffed Baked Potatoes

Prep. 20 min. Cook 55 min. Serves 8.

A perfect blend of robust flavors makes these potatoes unforgettable.

8 large baking potatoes
1 cup sour cream
½ teaspoon curry
½ teaspoon chives
½ teaspoon salt
½ teaspoon brown sugar
½ teaspoon cracked pepper
½ teaspoon real bacon bits
¼ cup butter, melted
½ cup milk

Scrub potatoes, prick with fork, and bake at 400° for 45 minutes or until tender. Cool, slit open, carefully scoop out pulp, and leave shells intact. Stir together sour cream, curry, chives, salt, sugar, pepper, and bacon bits. Combine with melted butter, milk, and potato pulp. Stuff into potato shells and bake at 375° for 10 minutes.

Make Ahead: Potatoes can be stuffed early in the day, refrigerated, and then baked at 375° for 10 minutes before serving. Stuffed potatoes can also be frozen (before final baking) on a tray until firm and then sealed in airtight wrap. Bake frozen at 350° for 30 minutes, or defrost and bake for 10 minutes at 375°.

Microwave: Halve recipe; scrub potatoes, prick with fork. Place in a circle like spokes in a wheel. Cook on high 16-19 minutes. If potatoes still feel firm, let stand in microwave 2-3 minutes. After stuffing, place in circle. Cook 5 minutes on high.

Healthy Potato Boats
Prep. 20 min. Cook 1 hour. Serves 4.

For convenience double this recipe, freeze, and store to have on hand for individual or group servings.

4 baking potatoes
1 egg, beaten
2 tablespoons milk
2 tablespoons butter or margarine
8 tablespoons Swiss cheese, grated
2 tablespoons minced onion
1 teaspoon thyme
½ teaspoon salt

Scrub potatoes, prick with fork, and bake at 400° for 45 minutes or until tender. Cool. Hollow out potatoes and leave skins intact. Mix pulp with beaten egg, milk, butter, cheese, onion, thyme, and salt. Fill skins with pulp mixture. Bake at 350° for 15 minutes.

Make Ahead: Before final baking, boats may be frozen on a tray until firm, then sealed in airtight wrap. Bake frozen at 350° for 30 minutes or defrost and bake at 375° for 10 minutes.

Microwave: Scrub potatoes; prick with fork. Place in a circle like spokes in a wheel. Cook on high 16-19 minutes. If potatoes still feel firm, allow to stand 2-3 minutes in microwave. After stuffing, place in circle, cook 5 minutes on high.

Creamy Potatoes
Prep. 10 min. Cook 30 min. Serves 4.

Smoother and creamier than Delmonico potatoes. Saves energy by cooking in a double boiler.

3 medium baking potatoes
½ teaspoon salt
1 bay leaf
1½ tablespoons grated onion
⅛ teaspoon garlic powder
½ cup grated cheddar cheese
¾ cup light cream
3 tablespoons butter or margarine

Peel and thinly slice potatoes. Cook them in boiling salted water with bay leaf for 3 minutes. Drain and place in top of double boiler. Sprinkle potatoes with onion, garlic powder, and cheese. Pour in cream and dot with butter. Cover pan and cook over moderately boiling water for about 30 minutes, or until potatoes are tender.

Rave Rice with Mushrooms
Prep. 20 min. Cook 10 min. Serves 8-10.

Count on people asking for seconds.

1 cup herb or wild rice
2¼ cups chicken stock (approximately)
5 cups quartered fresh mushrooms (1 pound)

1½ cups water
3 tablespoons butter or margarine
1 tablespoon flour
1 cup light cream
1 cup mushroom broth, reserved from
    mushroom cooking stock
Salt and pepper

Preheat oven to 350°. Cook rice according to package directions, but substitute the same amount of chicken stock for water.

Boil mushrooms in water in covered pan over medium heat for 10 minutes, then drain, but reserve 1 cup mushroom cooking broth. Brown mushrooms in 2 tablespoons butter.

Melt remaining 1 tablespoon butter, add flour, and cook over medium-low heat for 2 minutes while stirring constantly. Slowly add cream and broth. Continue cooking and stirring over medium-low heat until sauce is thickened and reduced to 1½ cups. Add salt and pepper to taste.

Put ⅓ of cooked rice in large greased casserole. Spread a third of mushrooms over rice and top with a third of the sauce. Repeat layers of rice, mushrooms, and sauce twice more, ending with sauce. Bake for about 10 minutes or until heated thoroughly.

Make Ahead: Cooked rice dish stays fresh in refrigerator for 2 days.

Desserts

Fruit, Mousse, Soufflés, Etc.

Grapes and Kirsch
Prep. 15 min. Serves 4.

Simple, refreshing summer dish with a subtle interplay of flavors.

1 ripe honeydew melon
1 cup fresh blueberries
1 cup seedless grapes
4 tablespoons kirsch
Sprinkling of confectioners sugar

Cut melon in half and remove seeds. Scoop out balls of melon, leaving shells intact. Mix melon balls with blueberries, grapes, and kirsch. Return fruit to shells and chill briefly. Sprinkle with sugar and serve from the melon shells.

Pineapple Garni
Prep. 15 min. Marinate 1 hr. Serves 4.

A sophisticated combination that is tasteful and unusual.

1 fresh ripe pineapple
4 tablespoons Grand Marnier

Trim off top and bottom of pineapple with a sharp knife. Cut off skin. Gouge out remaining "eyes" with point of knife. Slice into quarters, remove core, and cube remaining meat. Marinate with Grand Marnier for 1 hour. Serve in glass bowls. Juice is superb!

Note: It is quicker and looks fancier to cut pineapple into quarters from top through bottom. Then cut out core and cut meat neatly into bite-sized pieces leaving it in shell. Pour 1 tablespoon Grand Marnier over each quarter. Serve on plate. Served this way, the juices don't integrate as thoroughly, however.

Raspberry Bavarian
Prep. 10 min. Chill 3½ hr. Serves 6.

Cool, pretty, festive, and delightful. Recipe can be easily doubled.

1 package (3 ounces) raspberry jello
1 cup boiling water
¼ cup cold water
1 tablespoon lemon juice
1 teaspoon lemon rind
⅔ cup evaporated milk, chilled
1 cup raspberry yogurt
1 cup raspberries
½ cup raspberries for garnish
  (optional)

Dissolve jello in boiling water. Stir in cold water, lemon juice, and rind. Chill until partially set, about 30 minutes. Beat in milk until mixture is frothy and about double in volume. Add yogurt. Fold in 1 cup berries. Pour into sherbet glasses and chill until set, at least 3 hours. Garnish with half a cup of fresh berries if desired.

Quick Chocolate Pots de Crème
Prep. 5 min. Chill 4 hr. Serves 4.

Our favorite quick dessert. Make

multiples of recipe in separate batches.

1 egg
6 ounces semi-sweet chocolate chips
1½ tablespoons sugar, or 2 tablespoons crème de cacao, or 2 tablespoons Cointreau
1 teaspoon vanilla (omit if using liqueur)
Pinch of salt
¾ cup light cream

Put all ingredients except cream in blender. In small saucepan bring cream just to the boiling point (small bubbles will appear at the edge of the saucepan). Add hot cream to blender and blend for 1 minute on low until well blended. Pour into small cups and chill for at least 4 hours in the refrigerator or 1 hour in the freezer.

Make Ahead: Pots de crème are just as good after 2 days in refrigerator covered. They freeze well covered with airtight wrap. Defrost at room temperature.

Molded Chocolate Mousse
Prep. 30 min. Cool 30 min. Chill 4 hr. Serves 16.

A wonderful way to please a horde of Chocolate Lovers. Put it in your prettiest mold to decorate a buffet table.

2 envelopes unflavored gelatin
1 tablespoon water
4 eggs, separated
1⅓ cups milk
1 tablespoon instant coffee granules
½ cup sugar
12 ounces semi-sweet chocolate bits

1 teaspoon vanilla
½ cup sugar
2 cups heavy cream, whipped

Soften gelatin in water. Beat egg yolks and milk together until light and foamy. Cook yolk mixture, softened gelatin, coffee, ½ cup sugar, and chocolate chips over medium heat while stirring constantly. Without boiling, cook until gelatin is dissolved and chocolate is melted, about 5 minutes. Chill until mixture is thick (at least 30 minutes). Stir in vanilla.

Beat egg whites until soft peaks form. Gradually add ½ cup sugar and continue beating until stiff peaks form. Stir a third of whites into cooled chocolate mixture. Gently fold in rest of whites, being careful not to overmix. Fold in whipped cream. (Reserve a couple of tablespoons to decorate mold if desired.) Fill a lightly oiled 7-cup metal mold or number of molds totaling 7 cups. Fill each mold to top. Chill for at least 4 hours or overnight. Unmold and decorate with whipped cream.

Make Ahead: Mold stays fresh in refrigerator for a day. Do not freeze.

Note: To unmold, loosen sides with a knife, dip mold bottom into hot water, hold for 10 seconds, and invert onto plate. Or invert and cover metal mold with hot towels, or shake mold from side to side.

Eggnog Trifle
Prep. 35 min. Chill 8 hr. Serves 8-10.

Sinfully rich. An unusual combination of chocolate, rum, and custard.

10¾-ounce pound cake, frozen or fresh

2 bars (4 ounces each) sweet German chocolate
1 tablespoon dark rum
¼ cup water
1 tablespoon gelatin
2 tablespoons cold water
¾ cup butter or margarine
1 cup confectioners sugar
4 eggs, separated
2 tablespoons dark rum
¼ cup chopped almonds
¼ teaspoon cream of tartar
1 cup heavy cream
4 tablespoons confectioners sugar
2 teaspoons dark rum

Line a wide 2-quart bowl with thinly sliced pound cake. Melt chocolate in top of double boiler. Add 1 tablespoon rum and ¼ cup water. Stir until smooth. Spread over cake and cool in refrigerator.

Soak gelatin in 2 tablespoons water and dissolve over low heat. Set aside to cool *slightly* but not until gummy.

Cream butter and 1 cup confectioners sugar. Thoroughly beat in egg yolks and 2 tablespoons rum. Add nuts. Beat in dissolved gelatin, which should be slightly warm and *runny*. (Reheat if necessary.)

In separate bowl beat egg whites with cream of tartar until stiff, dry peaks are formed. Fold into butter-rum mixture. Pour into cooled cake-lined bowl. Chill until set — about 8 hours. Before serving, beat heavy cream until stiff, gradually adding 4 tablespoons confectioners sugar and 2 teaspoons rum while beating. Spread on top of trifle.

Double Orange Soufflé
Prep. 15 min. Cook 1 hr. Serves 6.

Let your dessert simmer while you enjoy dinner.

6 egg whites at room temperature
6 tablespoons sugar
6 tablespoons orange marmalade, not too sweet
2 tablespoons orange liqueur (Cointreau or Grand Marnier)
Sauce (see below)

Beat egg whites until soft peaks form. Gradually beat in 6 tablespoons sugar. Continue beating until stiff peaks form. Mix marmalade with liqueur and stir in a large spoonful of egg white. Then gently fold marmalade into remaining egg whites.

Butter the top pan and cover of a double boiler. Put soufflé into pan and cover it. Cook over simmering water for 1 hour, making sure water doesn't evaporate during cooking. Turn soufflé onto platter and serve promptly with sauce.

Sauce

½ cup butter
½ cup sugar
2 teaspoons medium cream
1 tablespoon vanilla
1 egg, well beaten

Cook butter, sugar, and cream over low heat, stirring occasionally, until butter is melted and sugar dissolved. Remove from heat, cool slightly, and add vanilla and beaten egg. Serve sauce in a separate bowl. Makes about ¾ cup.

Make Ahead: Sauce may be refrigerated for a day and gently reheated. It will be less foamy.

Chocolate Bombe
Prep. 20 min. Chill 1 hr. Serves 12.

An elegant ice cream pie and hot fudge sauce that can be made way ahead.

¼ cup butter
1½ cups crushed and packed chocolate sandwich cookies (about 18)
1 quart vanilla ice cream
1 quart chocolate ice cream
Hot Fudge Sauce (see below)

Melt butter and mix with cookie crumbs. Press in a *thin* layer on bottom and sides of a 9"-10" springform pan. Chill in freezer. Soften vanilla ice cream and spread it evenly over bottom crust, making sure ice cream reaches sides of pan. Freeze until firm, at least 20 minutes. Soften chocolate ice cream and spread over vanilla. Cover top with airtight plastic wrap and freeze. Shortly before serving, invert pan onto chilled serving dish and release sides. Cut into wedges and pass Hot Fudge Sauce separately.

Hot Fudge Sauce
Prep. 5 min. Cook 5 min. Makes 1½ cups.

Irresistible on other desserts as well.

1 cup sugar
¼ cup cornstarch
⅛ teaspoon salt
½ cup water
2 ounces unsweetened chocolate
½ cup light cream

Mix sugar, cornstarch, salt, and

water. Add chocolate and cook over medium heat, stirring constantly until chocolate melts. Add cream, bring to boil, and continue cooking for about a minute until sauce is thickened. Remove from heat.

Make Ahead: Frozen bombe covered with airtight wrap can be stored in freezer for a month. Fudge sauce stays fresh in refrigerator for a week. If necessary, over low heat, stir in some cream to thin sauce before serving.

Butter Almond Bombe

Prep. 20 min. Chill 1 hr. Serves 12.

This scrumptious ice cream pie topped with butterscotch sauce is another make-ahead favorite.

2 tablespoons butter
2 tablespoons amaretto liqueur
2 cups crushed macaroons
1 quart vanilla ice cream
1 quart butter almond ice cream
Butterscotch Sauce (see below)

Melt butter and mix with amaretto and crushed macaroons. Press in a *thin* layer evenly on bottom and sides of a 9″-10″ springform pan. Chill in freezer. Soften vanilla ice cream slightly and spread evenly over bottom crust, making sure ice cream reaches sides of pan. Freeze until firm. Soften butter almond ice cream and spread over vanilla. Cover top with airtight plastic wrap and freeze. Shortly before serving, invert onto chilled serving dish and release sides of pan. If necessary, slip knife carefully between pan bottom and crust to ease unmolding. Cut into wedges and accompany with Butterscotch Sauce.

Butterscotch Sauce

Prep. 5 min. Cook 6 min. Makes 2 cups.

This sauce keeps well for several weeks but it is doubtful it will hang around for that long.

⅔ cup white corn syrup
1¼ cups light brown sugar
4 tablespoons butter
½ teaspoon salt
1 teaspoon vanilla
½ cup whipping cream

In an enamel pan, use a wooden spoon to stir corn syrup, sugar, butter, and salt. Bring to a boil; heat to 224° on a candy thermometer. Cook for only 2 minutes. Cool, add vanilla and cream. Serve hot or cold.

Make Ahead: Frozen bombe, covered with airtight wrap, can be stored in freezer for a month. Sauce may be stored in refrigerator for several weeks. Heat in a double boiler to thin it.

Pineapple Rum Ice Cream

Prep. 15 min. Chill 1 hr. Serves 4.

Refreshingly different.

1 large, fresh pineapple
1 quart vanilla ice cream
1 to 2 ounces dark rum

Cut off top of pineapple and hollow out insides, leaving ¾″ of pineapple around perimeter. Save shell and top. Cut pineapple meat into small bite-sized chunks. Soften ice cream slightly and stir in rum and pineapple. Refreeze. Just before serving, fill shell with ice cream.

Coffee Ice Cream Mold
Prep. 10 min. Chill 1 hr. Serves 6.

A tantalizing blend of flavors. Unmold ahead of time and keep in freezer.

1 quart coffee ice cream
1 bottle (10 ounces) marron (chestnut) bits in vanilla
3 tablespoons crème de cacao

Chill 2-quart mold in freezer. Soften ice cream and fold in drained marrons and crème de cacao. Spread ice cream in mold, cover top with plastic wrap, and freeze.

To loosen, run a knife around sides of mold. If ice cream sticks, rub warm towel on bottom and sides of mold. Invert onto serving platter and put back in freezer until ready to serve.

Make Ahead: Frozen mold, covered in airtight wrap, can be stored in freezer for a month.

Zabaglione
Prep. 10 min. Cook 10 min. Serves 1.

A light foamy dessert which can easily be increased to serve more.

2 egg yolks
2 teaspoons sugar
4 tablespoons Marsala, rum, or sherry

Beat yolks and sugar until pale and frothy. Stir in wine. Heat in top of double boiler, stirring constantly until thickened. Pour into warmed glass.

Gogol Mogul
Prep. 10 min. Serves 1.

A Russian version of zabaglione.

2 egg yolks
3 teaspoons sugar
2 teaspoons rum or cognac

Add sugar to egg yolks and whip until thick and lemon colored. Add rum or cognac and serve immediately or let chill 30 minutes.

Cakes

Mrs. Erickson's Red Velvet Cake
Prep. 40 min. Cook 30 min. Serves 10.

This striking, moist, red cake came from an old friend's mother. Fun to serve on Valentine's Day in a heart-shaped pan.

½ cup butter or margarine
1½ cups sugar
2 eggs
2 teaspoons unsweetened cocoa
2 ounces red food coloring
1 cup buttermilk
2½ cups cake flour
1 teaspoon salt
1 teaspoon baking soda
1 teaspoon cider vinegar
1 teaspoon vanilla

Preheat oven to 350°. Cream butter, sugar, and eggs together. Mix in cocoa and food coloring. Add buttermilk alternately with flour and salt. Dissolve baking soda in vinegar and add with vanilla to batter. Beat thoroughly. Bake cake in 2 greased and floured 9" round cake pans for 30 minutes or until cake tester inserted in center comes out clean. Cool before removing from pans. Frost with White

Velvet Frosting (recipe follows).

Make Ahead: Freeze unfrosted cake in airtight wrap for up to 6 months. Freeze frosted cake until hard, wrap in foil, and store in freezer for up to 6 months. Unwrap before thawing.

Note: All-purpose flour can be substituted for cake flour, by using 3 tablespoons less of regular flour than amount of flour listed. However, cake will not rise as high.

White Velvet Frosting

Prep. 20 min. Makes enough for a 9″ two-layer cake.

A smooth, fluffy icing which goes well on Red Velvet Cake, Marble Cake, and Rich Chocolate Cake.

2 tablespoons flour, preferably "in-stantized" (like Wondra)
1 cup milk
1 cup sugar
1 cup margarine
1 teaspoon vanilla

Cook flour and milk in top of double boiler, stirring constantly, until very thick, about 10 minutes. Cool completely.

In separate bowl, cream sugar and margarine together until fluffy. Add vanilla. Beat in cooled flour mixture until sugar is no longer granular and frosting has consistency of whipped cream. This takes about 5 minutes.

Self-Frosted Chocolate Almond Cake

Prep. 10 min. Cook 30 min. Serves 12-14.

Easy to make but tastes as if it re-quired a lot of work. Pretty and luscious.

1 package (3.5 ounces) chocolate pudding (not instant)
1¾ cups milk
1 package (18.5 ounces) yellow or white cake mix
1 teaspoon almond flavoring (or 1 teaspoon vanilla if using cacao or Kahlua)
¼ cup amaretto (or crème de cacao or Kahlua)
6 ounces semi-sweet chocolate chips

Preheat oven to 350°. Cook pudding and milk over medium heat. Stir frequently until mixed and just about to a boil. Remove from heat. Allow to thicken and add to cake mix along with flavoring and liqueur. Beat until lumps dissolve.

Pour batter into greased and floured bundt pan or an 11″x7″ flat pan. Sprinkle chocolate chips on top of batter. Bake for 30-40 minutes until cake tester inserted in center comes out clean. If using bundt pan, cool cake for 10 minutes, loosen sides with a knife, and invert carefully onto a plate.

Make Ahead: Refrigerate for several days or freeze in airtight wrap for up to two months.

Kahlua Cheesecake

Prep. 50 min. Chill 4 hr. Serves 8-10.

A light, smooth, unusual cheesecake set off by a chocolate crust.

1⅔ cups crushed and packed chocolate sandwich cookies (about 20)
⅓ cup melted butter

2 eggs
½ cup sugar
1 teaspoon vanilla
1½ cups sour cream
1 pound softened cream cheese
1 tablespoon melted butter
3 tablespoons Kahlua (1 ounce)

Mix cookie crumbs and ⅓ cup melted butter. Press in a thin layer on bottom and sides of 9″-10″ greased springform pan and chill.

Put eggs, sugar, vanilla, and sour cream in blender or bowl of food processor and blend at high speed for a minute. Add cream cheese, cut in chunks, 1 tablespoon melted butter, and Kahlua and blend for another minute. Pour into crumb shell in springform pan and bake at 325° for 30-40 minutes or until custard is set. Filling should be soft; it will firm as it cools. Chill for 4 hours or overnight. Remove from pan carefully.

Hawaiian Carrot Cake
Prep. 30 min. Cook 1 hr. 15 min. Serves 10.

Macadamia nuts, pineapple, and coconut are a winning combination.

3 eggs
2 cups sugar
1½ cups vegetable oil
2 teaspoons vanilla
1 small can (8 ounces) crushed pineapple in juice
2 cups peeled, coarsely grated carrots
2½ cups cake flour (or 2½ cups less 3 tablespoons all-purpose flour)
1 teaspoon baking powder
1 teaspoon baking soda
1 teaspoon salt

1 teaspoon cinnamon
1 teaspoon nutmeg
1 cup coarsely chopped macadamia nuts (3½ ounces)
½ cup shredded coconut

Preheat oven to 350°. In a large mixing bowl, blend together eggs, sugar, and oil. Beat in vanilla, pineapple in juice, and carrots.

Sift flour, baking powder, soda, salt, cinnamon, and nutmeg together 3 times. Slowly add dry mixture to batter. Stir in chopped nuts and coconut. Bake in greased tube or large bundt pan for 1 hour 15 minutes. Frost with Coconut Icing (recipe follows) when cool.

Make Ahead: Unfrosted cake freezes well in airtight wrap for up to a month. Freeze frosted cake hard, wrap in foil, and return to freezer. Unwrap before thawing.

Coconut Icing
Prep. 10 min. Makes enough for one bundt cake.

Simple and delectable on Hawaiian Carrot Cake, Marble Cake, and Applesauce Cake.

4 tablespoons softened butter
4 tablespoons softened cream cheese
1 teaspoon vanilla
1½ cups sifted confectioners sugar
⅛ teaspoon salt
¼ cup coconut

Cream together butter and cream cheese until light. Beat in vanilla, sugar, and salt. Stir in coconut.

Marble Cake
Prep. 20 min. Cook 30 min. Serves 10-12.

A very high, moist, and pretty cake.

6 eggs
1 package (18.5 ounces) yellow or
   white cake mix
¾ cup vegetable oil
1 teaspoon vanilla
¼ cup buttermilk baking mix (like
   Bisquick)
¼ cup sour cream
½ cup semi-sweet chocolate bits
¼ teaspoon cream of tartar
¼ cup sugar

Separate eggs. Keep whites at room temperature. In a large bowl beat yolks, cake mix, oil, vanilla, and baking mix vigorously for 2 minutes. Mix in sour cream. Melt chocolate over low heat and set aside.

In a separate bowl, with clean, dry beater, whip egg whites until soft peaks form. *Gradually* beat in cream of tartar and sugar until stiff peaks form. Take 3 large spoonfuls of egg whites and mix well with batter to lighten it. Gently fold in remaining egg whites. Put a third of the batter in another bowl, stir in melted chocolate, and set aside.

Pour white batter into 2 well-greased and floured 9" layer cake pans. Pour chocolate batter on top of each. Run a knife through batter in a circular motion for a marbled effect. Bake in oven (not preheated) at 325° for 30-35 minutes. Do not overbake. Cake is done when a toothpick inserted in the center comes out clean. Cake crust will harden as it cools. Frost with 5-Minute Chocolate Icing (recipe follows).

Make Ahead: Wrap unfrosted cake in airtight wrap and freeze. Freeze frosted cake hard, wrap in foil, and freeze for up to 3-4 months. Unwrap before thawing.

5-Minute Chocolate Icing
Prep. 5 min. Makes enough for 9" two-layer cake.

Sour cream and chocolate mingle well in this fast frosting.

1½ cups semi-sweet chocolate bits
¾ cup sour cream
1 teaspoon vanilla

Melt chocolate bits and mix with sour cream and vanilla. Blend thoroughly.

Applesauce Cake
Prep. 15 min. Cook 30 min. Serves 9.

An old family recipe with excellent flavor.

½ cup softened butter
1 cup sugar
2 teaspoons baking soda
1½ cups flour
½ teaspoon cloves
1 teaspoon cinnamon
Dash of nutmeg
1⅓ cups unsweetened applesauce
1 cup raisins

Preheat oven to 350°. Cream butter and sugar together. Sift soda, flour, and spices into butter mixture. Blend well. Stir in applesauce and raisins. Pour batter into greased and floured 8" square pan. Bake for about 30 minutes or until a cake tester inserted in the center comes out clean. Cake is delicious plain or with Coconut Icing (p. 113).

Make Ahead: Freezes well in airtight wrap or stays fresh in refrigerator for 2 days.

Rich Chocolate Cake

Prep. 15 min. Cook 30 min. Serves 12.

Wickedly rich. Popular with kids of all ages.

1½ cups flour
2 cups sugar
1½ teaspoons baking soda
1 cup unsweetened cocoa
½ teaspoon salt
¾ cup vegetable oil
1½ cups water
2 teaspoons vanilla

Preheat oven to 350°. Sift dry ingredients into a bowl. Beat in liquids. Pour into greased 13"x9" pan. Bake for 30-35 minutes until cake tester inserted into center comes out clean. Frost with Fudge Mint Frosting (recipe follows) while cake is still warm or with White Velvet Frosting (p. 112).

Make Ahead: Cool cake, cover pan, and freeze for up to 4 months. Frosted cake may also be covered and frozen for up to 4 months. Unwrap before thawing.

Fudge Mint Frosting

Prep. 10 min. Makes enough for one oblong cake.

Extra chocolatey with a hint of mint. A smooth icing glaze which goes well on Rich Chocolate Cake, Marble Cake, and Fudge Brownies.

1 stick butter
3 tablespoons unsweetened cocoa
6 tablespoons milk
1 box (1 pound) confectioners sugar
½ teaspoon peppermint extract

In a large saucepan heat butter, cocoa, and milk to a boil while stirring. Sift sugar into a bowl. Beat in cocoa mixture and peppermint. Add more milk if icing is too thick.

Pies

French Apple Tarts

Prep. 20 min. Cook 1 hr. Makes 2 tarts.

A simple tart that looks festive and tastes terrific.

8 good-quality apples
2 unbaked pie shells (either 2 defrosted commercially frozen 9", or doubled recipe on p. 46)
3 eggs
⅔ cup sugar
1½ cups whole milk
2 teaspoons vanilla

Preheat oven to 350°. Core, peel, and quarter apples. Slice apples thinly by hand or with slicing blade of food processor. Attractively arrange apples in pie shells in overlapping concentric circles. Beat eggs and sugar together until foamy. Beat in milk and vanilla. Blend well. Pour one half of filling over apples in each crust. Bake for 1 hour. May be served warm or cold.

Strawberry Cheese Pie
Prep. 30 min. Bake 24 min. Chill 1 hr. Serves 8.

An impressive, cool summer pie. Strawberries and creamy cheese custard are a special combination.

11 ounces cream cheese
2 eggs
½ cup sugar
½ teaspoon vanilla
1 graham cracker pie crust for 9″ pie (2 cups graham cracker crumbs mixed with 5 tablespoons melted butter and pressed into buttered 9″ pie plate)
2 cups sour cream
¼ cup sugar
¼ cup sliced almonds (optional)
1 pint whole strawberries, hulled
4 tablespoons strawberry jelly
1 tablespoon water

Preheat oven to 350°. Beat cream cheese until smooth. Add eggs, one at a time, beating well after each addition. Gradually add ½ cup sugar and vanilla. Pour into graham crust and bake for 20 minutes.

Blend sour cream with ¼ cup sugar. Stir in almonds if desired. Spread mixture over pie. Turn off oven heat and return pie to oven for 4 minutes. Remove from oven and chill pie until set, about 1 hour.

Before serving, arrange whole strawberries on top of pie. Dissolve jelly in water over low heat. Pour over berries to glaze. Serve pie cold.

Midnight Mousse Pie
Prep. 25 min. Chill 2 hrs. Serves 6.

A rich, light, silky, chocolate treasure. Another good frozen asset.

4 ounces sweet German chocolate
2 tablespoons dark rum
1 tablespoon water
2 eggs
3 cups non-dairy frozen whipped topping, thawed (8 ounces)
Chocolate Crust (see below)

Melt chocolate with rum and water in top of double boiler. Stir until smooth. Cool in refrigerator. Add eggs, one at a time, beating for 4 minutes after each addition. Fold in whipped topping. Spoon mixture into prepared crust. Cover top with airtight wrap and freeze. Thaw at room temperature for 10 minutes before serving.

Chocolate Crust

¼ cup butter or margarine
1½ cups crushed and packed chocolate sandwich cookies

Melt butter and mix with cookie crumbs. Press into 9″ pie plate. Bake at 375° for 5 minutes.
Make Ahead: Entire pie or leftovers freeze for up to a month in airtight wrap.

Coconut Cream Pie
Prep. 30 min. Cook 15 min. Bake 15 min. Serves 6-8.

A light and pretty pie for all seasons.

3 eggs
⅓ cup sugar
¼ teaspoon salt

3 tablespoons cornstarch
1 tablespoon melted butter
2 cups milk or half-and-half
¾ cup grated coconut
1 teaspoon vanilla
Baked 9″ or 10″ pie shell (p. 46)
Meringue (see below)

Beat eggs until light. Continue beating while gradually adding sugar, salt, cornstarch, and melted butter. Heat milk or cream to the scalding point (bubbles around edges) and slowly beat it into the egg mixture. Cook in top of double boiler over slowly boiling water. Add coconut. Stir constantly, until mixture thickens to pudding consistency, about 10 minutes. Stir in vanilla. Pour into pie shell and chill thoroughly. Top with meringue.

Meringue

2 egg whites, at room temperature
¼ teaspoon cream of tartar
⅛ teaspoon salt
4 tablespoons extra-fine sugar
½ teaspoon vanilla
¼ cup coconut

Beat egg whites until stiff. Slowly beat in cream of tartar, salt, sugar, and vanilla. Spread over pie, bringing meringue to edge of crust so it does not pull away while cooking. Sprinkle with coconut. Bake at 300° for 15 minutes.

Microwave: Bake on high for 3½ minutes, rotating ¼ turn every 30 seconds.

Deluxe Banana Cream Pie

Prep. 30 min. Cook 15 min. Bake 15 min. Serves 6-8.

Meringue topping balances and enhances the banana flavor.

3 eggs
⅓ cup sugar
¼ teaspoon salt
3 tablespoons cornstarch
1 tablespoon melted butter
2 cups milk or half-and-half
1 teaspoon vanilla
2 ripe bananas, thinly sliced
Baked 9″ or 10″ pie shell (p. 46)
Meringue (recipe follows)

Beat eggs until light. Continue beating while gradually adding the sugar, salt, cornstarch, and melted butter. Heat milk or cream to the scalding point and slowly add to the egg mixture while beating continuously. Cook in top of double boiler over slowly boiling water; stir constantly until mixture thickens to pudding consistency, about 10 minutes. Stir in vanilla and bananas. Pour into pie shell and chill thoroughly. Top with meringue.

Meringue

2 egg whites, at room temperature
¼ teaspoon cream of tartar
⅛ teaspoon salt
4 tablespoons extra-fine sugar
½ teaspoon vanilla

Beat egg whites until stiff. Slowly beat in cream of tartar, salt, sugar, and vanilla. Cover pie with meringue, spreading it to the edge of the crust so it does not pull away while cooking.

Bake at 300° for 15 minutes.

Microwave. Bake on high for 3½ minutes, rotating ¼ turn every 30 seconds.

Fresh Strawberry Pie
Prep. 15 min. Chill 2 hr. Serves 8.

Raises the strawberry to new heights.

1 quart ripe, hulled strawberries
2 tablespoons confectioners sugar
9″ fully baked pie shell, homemade (p. 46) or frozen
¾ cup water
1 cup white sugar
3 tablespoons cornstarch
½ teaspoon cinnamon
1 teaspoon lemon juice
Topping (optional), see below

Sprinkle all but 1 cup of berries with 2 tablespoons confectioners sugar; line cooled shell with sugared berries.

Cook the cup of reserved berries in water for 3-4 minutes until slightly limp. Mix 1 cup white sugar, cornstarch, and cinnamon together. Cook sugar mixture and cooked fruit together, stirring constantly until thick and clear in color, about 5-10 minutes. Add lemon juice. Cool slightly and pour over sugared berries in shell. Chill.

Topping (optional)

1 cup heavy cream
4 tablespoons confectioners sugar
½ teaspoon vanilla

Just before serving, if desired, whip cream and fold in confectioners sugar and vanilla. Spread over chilled pie or pass separately in bowl.

Note: If using frozen crust, bake according to package directions. For homemade crust, prick with fork, put bottom-greased pie plate on top to hold it down, and bake at 400° for 5 minutes. Remove inside plate and continue baking for 7-10 minutes more, until golden brown.

Make Ahead: Pie may be made a day ahead and stored without whipped cream in the refrigerator.

Rum Pumpkin Chiffon Pie
Prep. 25 min. Chill 3 hrs. Serves 8.

A superior form of the prosaic pumpkin pie. A grand finale for Thanksgiving dinner.

1 envelope unflavored gelatin
¾ cup dark brown sugar
½ teaspoon salt
½ teaspoon nutmeg
1 teaspoon cinnamon
½ cup milk
3 eggs, separated
1½ cups canned plain pumpkin
⅓ cup dark rum
¼ cup white sugar
9″ graham cracker pie crust (See Strawberry Cheese Pie, p. 116)
1 cup heavy cream (optional)

Mix gelatin, brown sugar, salt, nutmeg, and cinnamon in a saucepan. Stir in milk, egg yolks, and pumpkin. Cook over medium heat, stirring constantly, until gelatin is dissolved, about 10 minutes. Remove from heat, add rum, and chill for about 2 hours. Mixture should mound slightly when lifted with a spoon. Stir occasionally.

Beat egg whites at room temperature until soft peaks form. Beat in ¼ cup white sugar and continue beating until stiff peaks form. Fold into gelatin mixture. Put in pie shell and chill for another hour.

If desired, whip cream and spread on pie shortly before serving.

Make Ahead: Pie freezes well in airtight wrap. Thaw at room temperature before serving.

Index

About the Authors

Judy Duncan and Allison McCance are lifelong friends who have two all-consuming passions in common — cooking and playing tennis. Figuring out how to save time in the kitchen so as to have more time on the courts was the motivating force behind this book. They have written it for the active person who wants to prepare good food and entertain with style, but also have ample time for other pursuits, interests, and responsibilities.

Mrs. Duncan started cooking as a young girl, when her family's Swedish cook introduced her to basic cooking techniques and preparations. Trips abroad exposed her to foods and ingredients from all parts of the world, which in turn inspired an ongoing interest in experimenting with new flavor combinations. She lives in Sherborn, Massachusetts, with her husband and two daughters, whom she describes as a patient family who appreciate her efforts in the kitchen and thrive on the variety of her menus.

Allison McCance discovered her interest in cooking right after she graduated from college and began poring over countless cookbooks and magazine articles for recipe ideas. She soon learned how to divide her time between family, a research job at Harvard Business School, and sports, and became expert at inventing shortcuts — whether for preparing a meal or planning a party. Mrs. McCance, who lives with her husband and daughter in Westwood, Massachusetts, has managed her time well enough to have been ranked #1 in New England tennis doubles.